HOW
VIRTUAL
REALITY
WORKS

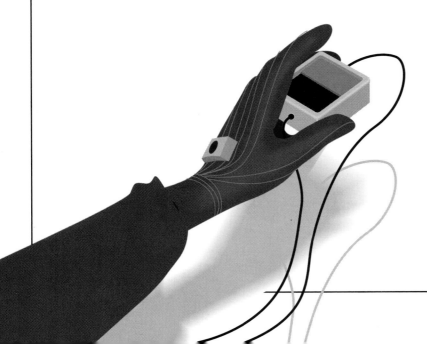

HOW VIRTUAL REALITY WORKS

JOSHUA EDDINGS

Illustrated by
PAMELA DRURY WATTENMAKER

Ziff-Davis Press
Emeryville, California

Development Editor	Valerie Haynes Perry
Copy Editor	Kate Hoffman
Technical Reviewer	Linda Jacobson
Technical Consultant	Louis M. Brill
Project Coordinator	Barbara Dahl
Proofreader	Carol Burbo
Cover Illustration	Regan Honda and Pamela Drury Wattenmaker
Cover Design	Carrie English
Series Book Design	Carrie English
Illustrator	Pamela Drury Wattenmaker
Word Processing	Howard Blechman
Page Layout	M.D. Barrera and P. Diamond
Indexer	Valerie Robbins

Ziff-Davis Press books are produced on a Macintosh computer system with the following applications: FrameMaker®, Microsoft® Word, QuarkXPress®, Adobe Illustrator®, Adobe Photoshop®, Adobe Streamline™, MacLink®*Plus*, Aldus® FreeHand™, Collage Plus™.

If you have comments or questions or would like to receive a free catalog, call or write:
Ziff-Davis Press
5903 Christie Avenue
Emeryville, CA 94608
1-800-688-0448

ISBN 1-56276-230-3

Manufactured in the United States of America
This book is printed on paper that contains 50% total recycled fiber of which 20% is de-inked postconsumer fiber.
10 9 8 7 6 5 4 3 2

For Regina and M. Natalio

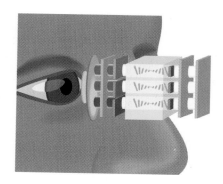

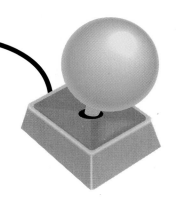

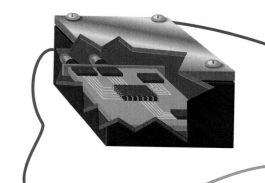

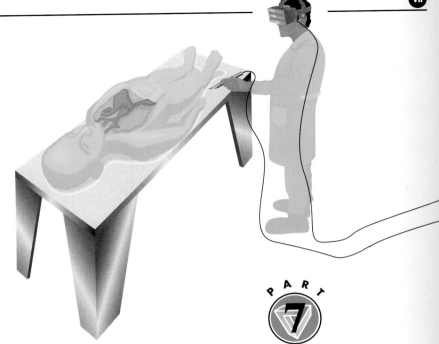

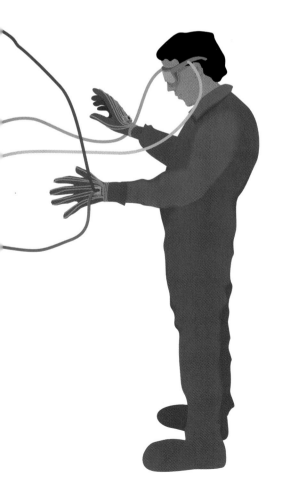

Thanks to Valerie Haynes Perry, development editor at Ziff-Davis Press, for her help in completing this book in time to make the deadline. And thanks to Pamela Drury Wattenmaker, illustrator. I am amazed at how she is able to read my mind to capture the essence of my sketches. And special thanks to the rest of the editorial and production team for this project: Kate Hoffman, copy editor; Barbara Dahl, project coordinator; Howard Blechman, word processor; and M.D. Barrera and P. Diamond, layout artists.

I also greatly appreciate the information that Dr. Dean Inman of the Oregon Research Institute provided me on his work with disabled children.

Kathy Henley's support and assistance in writing the sections on education and disabilities were also of great value to me.

I am grateful for the ideas and input that technical reviewers Louis Brill and Linda Jacobson provided.

And, as imagination bodies forth
The forms of things unknown, the poet's pen
Turns them to shapes, and gives to airy nothing
A local habitation and a name

—William Shakespeare, A Midsummer Night's Dream

Shakespeare wasn't describing virtual reality, but his words capture its essence. Virtual reality, or VR, allows human imagination to create shapes and sounds out of invisible electrons racing through circuits. Like the poets to whom Shakespeare alludes, science fiction writers have long imagined the virtual worlds that we can now explore due to the development of this very sophisticated twentieth-century technology.

Virtual reality is the new poet's pen, a computer tool that turns imagination and thought into simulations, virtual worlds, habitats of airy nothing that appear real to our senses. These worlds are places where we can both work and play.

This book will provide you with a good definition of the term "virtual reality." In addition to tracing the electronic developments that laid the groundwork for VR technology, *How Virtual Reality Works* also discusses how our senses work. This foundation is important to understanding the ways in which VR systems seek to effectively engage our senses when we are within a virtual world. Once that understanding is established, the discussion turns to specific hardware and software considerations.

Immersion and interactivity are the two criteria on which VR simulations are based. Immersion refers to the ability of participants to believe they are "present" in the virtual world and can navigate through and function within the simulation as if it were physical reality. Interactivity pertains to the participant's ability to manipulate objects encountered within a virtual world. Various degrees of experience are possible within a simulation, depending on the hardware and software. Desktop VR, fully immersive environments, and augmented reality will be discussed in the context of the respective degree of experience that each offers.

You may be most familiar with recreational examples of VR. However, VR technology is being applied in professional fields as well. This book describes examples of such applications in the fields of medicine, architecture and engineering, the military, science, and financial analysis.

What does the future of VR technology hold? In addition to research that is being done and applied in the fields of communication, engineering, and medicine, there is great potential for applications in the field of education. In fact, education may prove the most fertile ground for future growth, given the potential of VR technology to link students worldwide. Imagine a world in which knowledge can be shared in real time within simulations that can integrate information that spans the course of history. Imagine being able to interact with simulations of historical figures in a networked, virtual world. Imagine learning from their successes and failures. Just imagine.

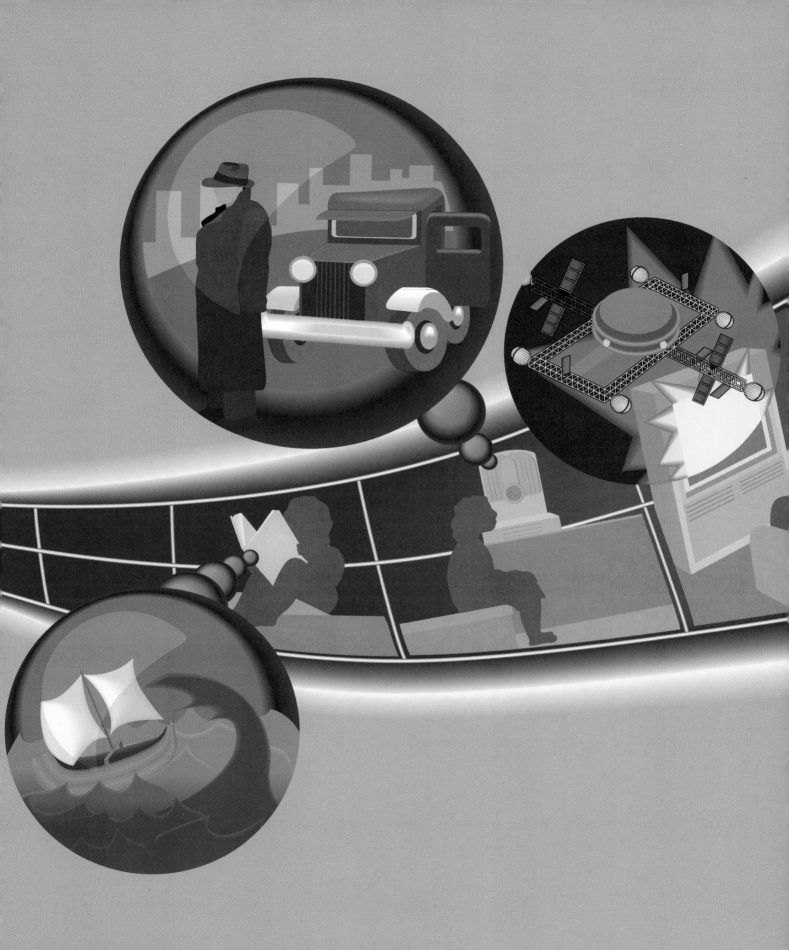

WHAT IS VIRTUAL REALITY?

CONTENTS

OVERVIEW

VIRTUAL REALITY (VR) is the use of computers and other special hardware and software to generate a simulation of an alternate world. One world could be a place of learning. Another could consist of games and adventure. Yet another could simulate a workplace, and so on. A participant interacts with the simulation through his or her senses. Sight and sound are the senses that are typically engaged.

Today's VR hardware and software are hardly the final word in this sophisticated technology. In fact, the hardware and software evolve every few months. However, the principles that VR is based upon do not change; they are almost etched into our genetic code because they capitalize on our senses. If we examine how our brains integrate our entire range of sensory data, we can understand what VR hardware and software seek to accomplish. Science fiction writers can make accurate projections of things to come largely because they extrapolate from these constant sensory processes.

A blending of imagination and technology makes VR possible. Roger Bacon's thirteenth century scientific musings about horseless carriages and powered machinery offer early evidence of this "blending"; and Jules Verne wrote futuristic fiction in the 1800s about rockets and submarines. Science fiction writers in particular have made projections that have become embodied in the concepts behind VR. And Hollywood has used computers and television to introduce and reinforce some of these projections.

There are several technological milestones that have been achieved within the last hundred years that have made VR possible. The telephone, radio, and TV; the evolution of semiconductors from diodes into transistors and integrated circuits; the development of integrated circuits into microprocessor chips and liquid crystal displays; the ongoing miniaturization of electronics; and the rapid evolution of computer power have all contributed to the development of VR technology. Early attempts at simulations, including the first flight simulator, the Sensorama arcade ride, 3-D movies, and video games were all precursors to today's VR simulations.

Science Fiction versus Virtual Reality

SCIENCE FICTION LITERATURE has been a worthy vehicle for authors who speculate about better ways for mind and machine to work together. Sometimes technology catches up with this speculation, though not always in the fashion science fiction authors imagine.

Such is the case with virtual reality (VR), a term that describes a very sophisticated mind-machine interace. Many consider William Gibson's description of cyberspace in his book *Neuromancer*, published in 1984, to be the ultimate virtual reality. *Cyberspace* is the sum of all interconnected telecommunication networks in Gibson's future world. People enter, or *jack into,* cyberspace by plugging a cable from a computer into a socket hard-wired into their brains. Once jacked in, a person experiences cyberspace directly, and a whole new set of electronic stimuli replace the sensations of the real world.

Hollywood was quick to pick up the banner of science fiction to popularize VR. Hollywood uses the visual magic of special effects to imitate VR systems. However, TV programs and films are not examples of actual VR. TV and films are not customized for individual participants nor are they interactive; both of these factors are basic to VR simulations.

The TV series *Star Trek: The Next Generation* is a specific example of how Hollywood has used science fiction to popularize VR. In this program, the holodeck is a room on the Starship Enterprise that uses twenty-fourth-century technology to generate artificial worlds. The Enterprise crew can explore places such as Romulan solar systems, French cafes, and Sherwood Forest, without ever physically leaving the holodeck.

The holodeck is a classic example of a VR system that supports immersion, which is an essential aspect of creating VR simulations. *Immersion* refers to the system's ability to make a person feel "immersed" in the computer-generated simulation. This is accomplished in the holodeck without requiring the participant to wear any VR input and output devices, such as gloves and helmuts.

The Evolution of Imagination

Radio brought a new element to storytelling: spontaneous, real-time (that is, live) audiences spread over a large geographical area. Sound effects could also accompany stories. People relied on the sense of hearing to be transported into an imaginary world that only existed in their minds.

Even the earliest stories, told around campfires with props of animal fur and feathers, allowed people to suspend their disbelief and enter into a shared world of imagination. Books became a medium for stories to travel over vast distances of space and time. A reader can enter into the world of the ancient Greek mythology or into the world of present day authors.

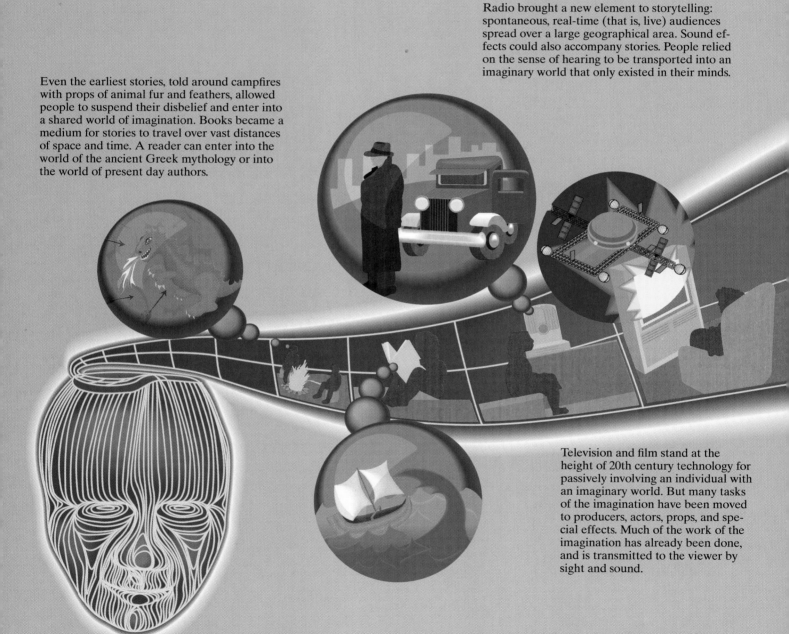

Television and film stand at the height of 20th century technology for passively involving an individual with an imaginary world. But many tasks of the imagination have been moved to producers, actors, props, and special effects. Much of the work of the imagination has already been done, and is transmitted to the viewer by sight and sound.

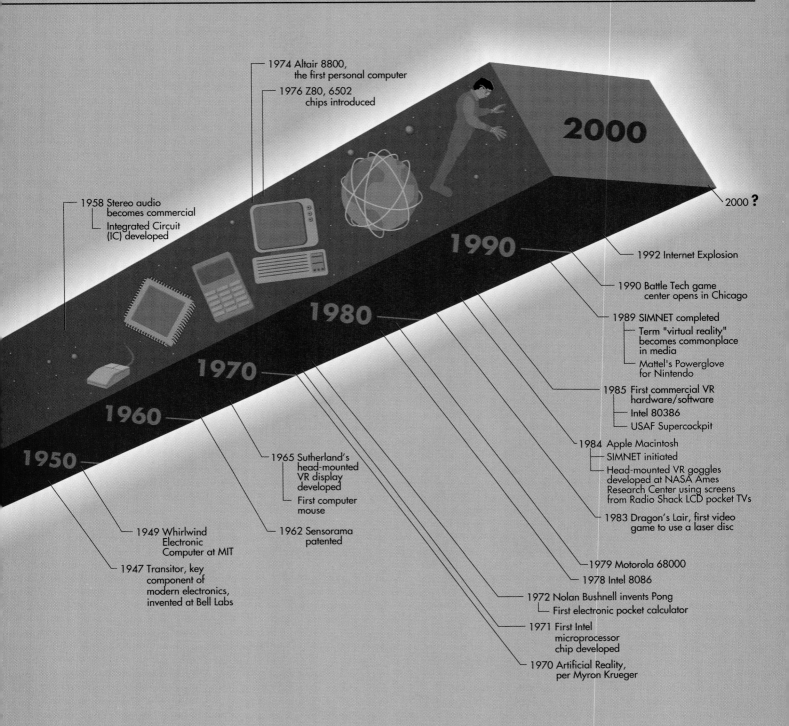

1974 Altair 8800,
the first personal computer

1976 Z80, 6502
chips introduced

2000

1958 Stereo audio
becomes commercial

Integrated Circuit
(IC) developed

2000 **?**

1990

1992 Internet Explosion

1990 Battle Tech game
center opens in Chicago

1980

1989 SIMNET completed

Term "virtual reality"
becomes commonplace
in media

Mattel's Powerglove
for Nintendo

1970

1985 First commercial VR
hardware/software

Intel 80386

USAF Supercockpit

1960

1984 Apple Macintosh

SIMNET initiated

Head-mounted VR goggles
developed at NASA Ames
Research Center using screens
from Radio Shack LCD pocket TVs

1950

1965 Sutherland's
head-mounted
VR display
developed

First computer
mouse

1983 Dragon's Lair, first video
game to use a laser disc

1949 Whirlwind
Electronic
Computer at MIT

1962 Sensorama
patented

1979 Motorola 68000

1978 Intel 8086

1947 Transitor, key
component of
modern electronics,
invented at Bell Labs

1972 Nolan Bushnell invents Pong

First electronic pocket calculator

1971 First Intel
microprocessor
chip developed

1970 Artificial Reality,
per Myron Krueger

2

ENGAGING THE SENSES

CONTENTS

OVERVIEW

F VIRTUAL REALITY is based on the interface between mind and machine, our senses and how they work are central to VR.

Our brains allow us to perceive the exterior, physical world. A VR system processes and displays a *simulated* world, presenting it to the senses through VR output devices. A VR *output device* changes electronic signals into physical phenomena. A VR *input device* measures and records physical phenomena electronically, creating digital signals that the computer understands. Ultimately, VR input and output devices seek to provide sense data that the brain can interpret.

Our senses are the data channels between the outside world and the brain. All the senses rely on specialized receptors that translate into nerve impulses physical phenomena such as sound waves, light, or heat. These nerve impulses move along the pathways of the nervous system to specific areas of the brain. The visual cortex is an example of one area of the brain that is actually a complex signal processor. It transforms nerve impulses into information the brain can interpret.

To provide appropriate output, VR systems need to receive input from the participant. Input devices for VR systems range from traditional computer keyboards and mice to more unusual navigation and interaction devices developed specifically for virtual reality, such as position trackers. Speech recognition is an exciting potential VR input technology. It would allow the participant to speak into a microphone connected to a computer, bypassing the need to use a keyboard or other manual device for entering data. The computer would then translate the spoken words into a stream of commands, just as if they had been typed. Current speech recognition systems come nowhere near the sophistication of the computer "HAL" in the science fiction movie *2001: A Space Odyssey*. Not only could HAL recognize spoken words, he could also read lips!

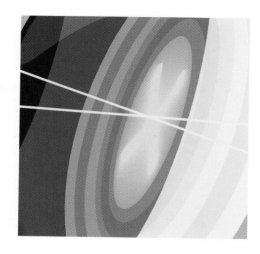

CHAPTER

3

How Vision Works

OUR EYES ARE a complex gateway between the physical world and our brains, which process visual information. To comprehend the role sight plays in VR simulations, we need to explore how vision works. We also need to know something about the types of visual information our eyes convey to our brains.

In the real world, we can see objects that are illuminated by the sun, or by light from artificial sources such as candles or electric lights. We actually see waves of light that are bounced or reflected off the illuminated object. The lens of the eye gathers this reflected light and refracts it onto the back of the eyeball, which is also called the *retina*. *Rods* and *cones*, neural receptors within the retina, change this light into nerve impulses. These impulses pass through the optic nerve to the *visual cortex*, the area of the brain where the nerve impulses are turned into the images we see.

When we look at objects, we see colors and shapes, and we perceive depth and movement. Illustrators take these factors into account when producing VR images for computer graphics. Furthermore, most of us have *stereoscopic* vision, which means each eye sees the same three-dimensional object or scene from a slightly different vantage point. The brain combines the slightly different views into one stereoscopic view. Stereoscopic vision also helps provide depth perception, which is a key element in creating realistic landscapes with computer graphics.

A VR display device's basic task is to transform a computer-generated signal into visible light, and to direct and focus that light onto the eyes. The device facilitates the replacement of objects we see in the real world with objects that are part of a computer-generated world. Here's how this happens. Instead of receiving the reflected light waves from the real world, the eyes receive an alternate set of light waves generated by the VR display device, which the brain can also interpret and allow us to see.

A computer screen is the simplest VR display device. Stereoscopic glasses are often used with computer screens to provide a stereoscopic picture. Head-mounted displays (HMDs) that provide a separate image for each eye are sophisticated VR display devices. Most HMDs use liquid crystal display (LCD) screens and special optics to provide the images for each eye.

The Eye

Sunlight illuminates objects, allowing us to see them. An illuminated object reflects rays of light and the human eye changes light into nerve impulses that our brain can see. The eye refracts light onto the retina, where rods and cones change the light to nerve impulses.

OVERLAPPING

Each of our eyes provides slightly different views of any given scene or object we observe. The visual cortex interprets these views and combines them into a single stereoscopic scene.

FIELD OF VIEW

A pair of human eyes is arranged to accommodate a *field of view* that is about 220° wide. But vision is not uniform over this entire field. The stereoscopic field of view in which objects appear three-dimensional because of depth perception is much smaller.

The visual cortex is the part of the brain that processes nerve impulses from the eyes, allowing us to see.

Optic nerve

Visual cortex

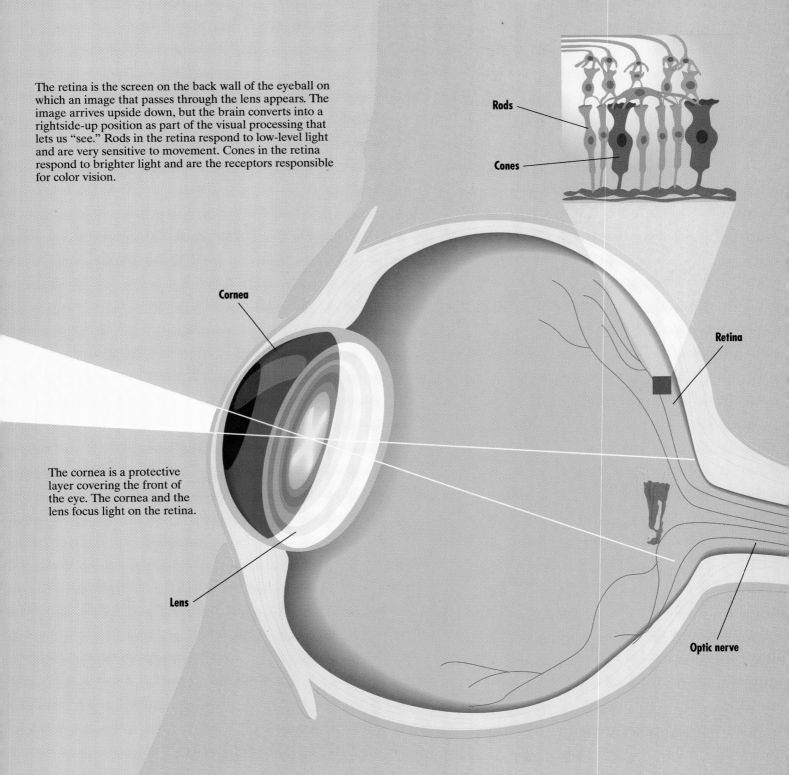

The retina is the screen on the back wall of the eyeball on which an image that passes through the lens appears. The image arrives upside down, but the brain converts into a rightside-up position as part of the visual processing that lets us "see." Rods in the retina respond to low-level light and are very sensitive to movement. Cones in the retina respond to brighter light and are the receptors responsible for color vision.

Rods

Cones

Cornea

Retina

The cornea is a protective layer covering the front of the eye. The cornea and the lens focus light on the retina.

Lens

Optic nerve

VR Display Devices

A variety of display devices convert computer signals into images. The computer monitor is the simplest display device. A computer monitor can generate two separate images that appear as a single stereoscopic 3-D image when the observer views them while wearing special stereoscopic glasses. VR goggles are sophisticated VR head-mounted display devices. They provide distinct images to each eye.

Computer monitors are based on cathode ray technology, which is similar to the technology used in television sets. A stream of electrons is generated in an electron gun. The electrons are swept across the screen, which is coated with phosphors. The phosphors glow when struck by electrons. A color image is "painted" on the screen by using three electron guns, each pointed at a type of phosphor that glows a different color.

3-D glasses, with blue and red filters for lenses, are sometimes used with a monitor to create a stereoscopic effect. Two images—one red, one blue—are generated on the screen, placed a fraction of an inch apart. When you look at a 3-D picture without the special glasses, you see a very fuzzy picture, because the images are not lined up exactly. When you put on a pair of 3-D glasses, each eye sees only one of the images, so the visual cortex is presented with two views of the same image. The visual cortex then recombines the images into a 3-D view.

Liquid crystal displays (LCDs) use long liquid crystals to create an image. Liquid crystals change their physical orientation when an electrical charge is applied to them. There are thousands of liquid crystals in a LCD screen, all changing position many times a second. LCDs use polarizing filters, which only allow light oriented in one direction to pass through the filter. Light waves become oriented to the normal resting place of the liquid crystals. When a charge is applied to a crystal, the orientation changes and blocks out that ray of light. Color filters can be used with additional layers of crystals to create color displays. Using a pair of liquid crystal shutter glasses is a more sophisticated way to generate a stereoscopic display. Two separate views of the same scene are generated and each view is displayed on the same screen many times per second. The shutters on each side of the glasses are linked to one of the views, so the shutter only opens when the related view is on the screen. The shutter closes when the other view is displayed. When this happens at least 60 times a second, the brain combines both images into a single stereoscopic view.

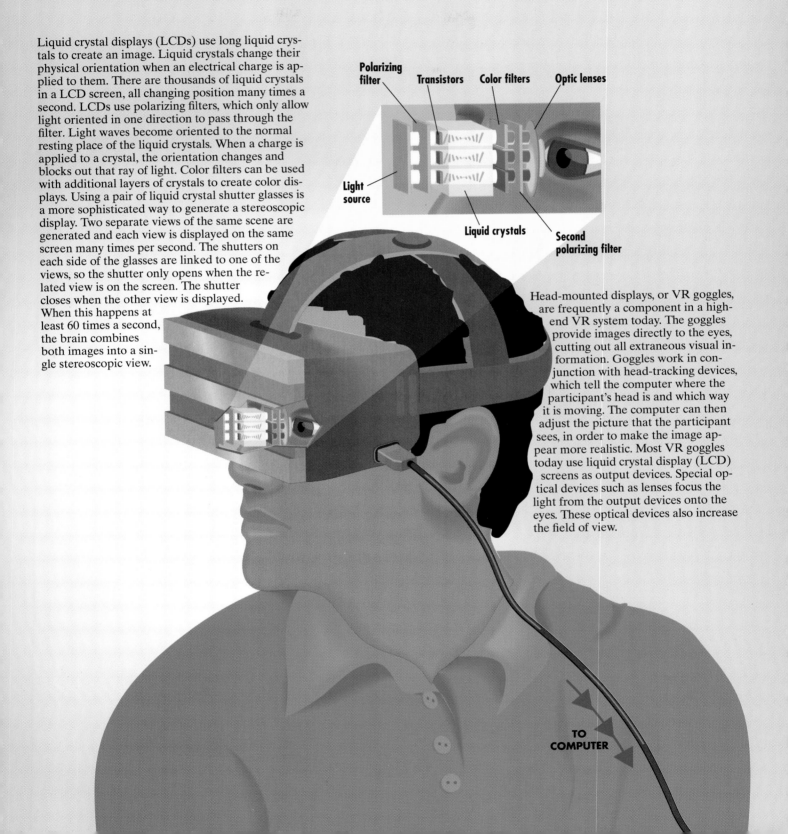

Polarizing filter **Transistors** **Color filters** **Optic lenses**

Light source

Liquid crystals **Second polarizing filter**

Head-mounted displays, or VR goggles, are frequently a component in a high-end VR system today. The goggles provide images directly to the eyes, cutting out all extraneous visual information. Goggles work in conjunction with head-tracking devices, which tell the computer where the participant's head is and which way it is moving. The computer can then adjust the picture that the participant sees, in order to make the image appear more realistic. Most VR goggles today use liquid crystal display (LCD) screens as output devices. Special optical devices such as lenses focus the light from the output devices onto the eyes. These optical devices also increase the field of view.

TO COMPUTER

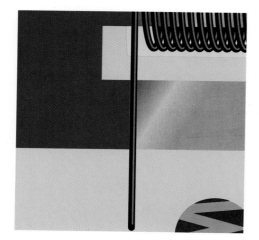

CHAPTER 4

How Sound Works

THE HUMAN EAR is the sensory organ that turns sound waves into signals the brain can interpret. The brain can determine the approximate distance and direction of any sounds the ears receive. The brain can then place the sounds that it interprets into a mental map that corresponds to the simultaneous visual image the eyes receive. To comprehend the role sound plays in virtual reality simulations, we need to know something about the types of audio information our ears convey to our brains.

Sound greatly enhances a VR system's ability to make us feel that we are immersed in another world. Sound consists of vibrating waves; anything we hear is the result of sound waves that were generated by some type of vibration.

The outer ear gathers sound waves and guides them into the ear canal. These waves make the eardrum vibrate. The eardrum is connected to the middle ear and the inner ear. Within the inner ear, sound waves are transformed into nerve impulses. These impulses are sent to the cerebral cortex, the area of the brain that interprets the nerve signals from both ears into noise, spoken language, music, or positional clues which help the brain place a sound within a given setting.

An audio output device changes electrical signals into sound. These devices use electromagnetic speakers to generate sound waves. The speakers may be external or contained in headphones. An electrical signal is converted into mechanical movement, which causes a diaphragm within the speaker or headphone to vibrate. This diaphragm's movement creates sound waves in the air.

Stereo sound (or two channels of sound) is an important component in an effective VR simulation. A VR system can generate two or more channels of sounds, to replace the sounds of the real world each ear hears. This type of audio simulation requires careful tracking of the time delay between sounds for each ear. A high-quality sound localization system is essential for achieving this effect.

Sound can make a simulation more believable. It can be used to send warnings, to provide music or special effects, and to synthesize computer messages into a human-sounding voice. Work has also been done toward enabling computers to recognize human speech. Two-way sound devices already allow conversation between humans and computers in research labs.

The Ear

This sensory organ translates into nerve impulses the myriad of sounds in our world that the brain can interpret. There are many sources of sound waves in our world: planes, birds, traffic, music, the wind, the human voice, and so on. Sound waves are nothing more than vibrations that pass through the air and other media, such as water or solid materials.

Each of our two ears hears the same sound a little differently. The sound may be stronger in one ear, and may arrive a fraction of a second before the other ear detects it. The brain can automatically interpret the sounds it receives from the ears, and so "place" the origin of a sound in relationship to the head.

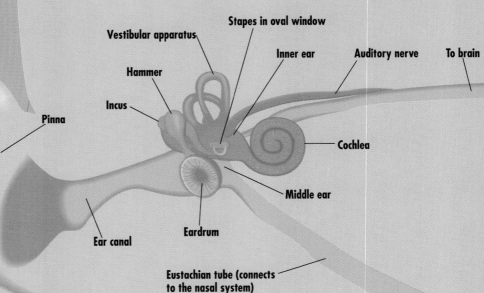

Stapes in oval window

Vestibular apparatus

Inner ear

Auditory nerve

To brain

Hammer

Incus

Pinna

Cochlea

Middle ear

Eardrum

Ear canal

Eustachian tube (connects
to the nasal system)

The ear changes sound waves into
nerve impulses. The *pinna*, or outer
ear, gathers sound waves and guides
them into the ear canal. These waves
make the eardrum vibrate. The eardrum is
connected to the middle ear, which consists of three small
bones called the *hammer*, the *incus*, and the *stapes*. These
bones focus direct sound vibrations to the inner ear or
cochlea. The vibrations are then transferred into waves in
the fluid contained in the inner ear and the *vestibular
apparatus*, which affects balance and the position of the
body. Waves in the fluid within the inner ear move sensory
hairs that are connected to auditory nerve cells that convert movement of the sensory hairs into nerve impulses.
These impulses are sent to the cerebral cortex, which interprets nerve signals from both ears into the "sounds" the
brain hears.

Audio Systems

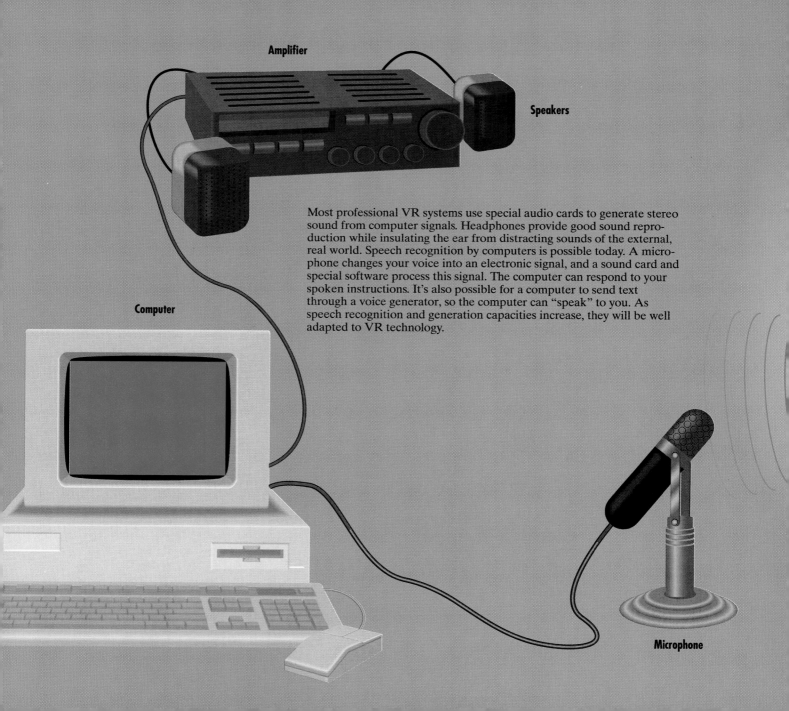

Amplifier

Speakers

Computer

Most professional VR systems use special audio cards to generate stereo sound from computer signals. Headphones provide good sound reproduction while insulating the ear from distracting sounds of the external, real world. Speech recognition by computers is possible today. A microphone changes your voice into an electronic signal, and a sound card and special software process this signal. The computer can respond to your spoken instructions. It's also possible for a computer to send text through a voice generator, so the computer can "speak" to you. As speech recognition and generation capacities increase, they will be well adapted to VR technology.

Microphone

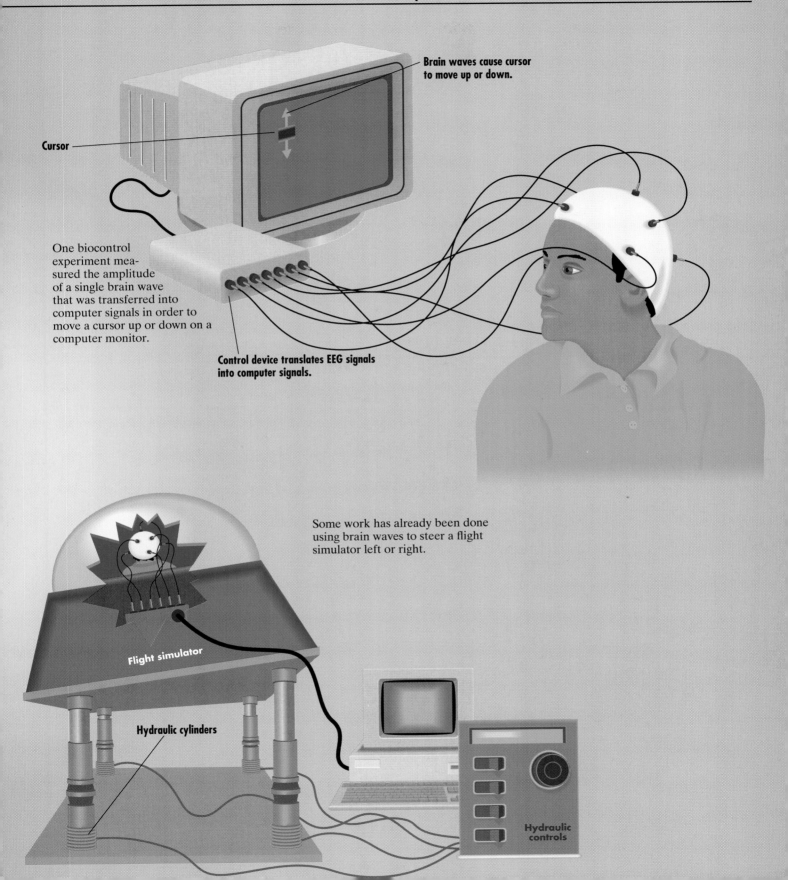

Brain waves cause cursor
to move up or down.

Cursor

One biocontrol
experiment mea-
sured the amplitude
of a single brain wave
that was transferred into
computer signals in order to
move a cursor up or down on a
computer monitor.

Control device translates EEG signals
into computer signals.

Some work has already been done
using brain waves to steer a flight
simulator left or right.

Flight simulator

Hydraulic cylinders

Hydraulic
controls

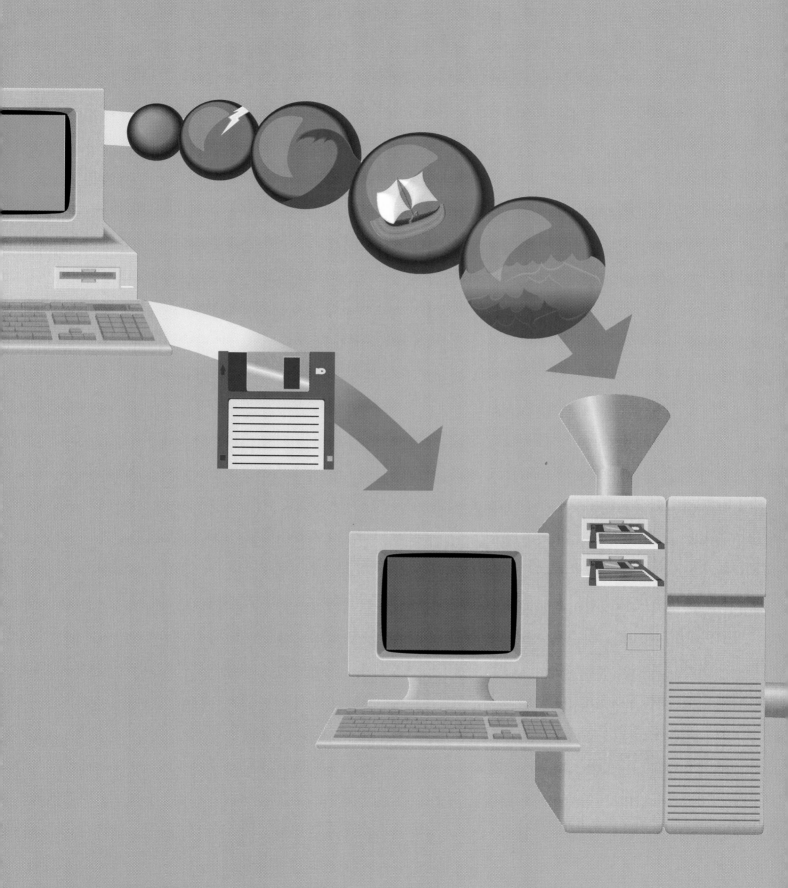

HARDWARE AND SOFTWARE

CONTENTS

OVERVIEW

VIRTUAL REALITY SYSTEMS, like other types of computer systems, rely on hardware and software to build simulations. Personal computers, workstations, or supercomputers are examples of the types of hardware required to produce simulations. Input and output devices also fall under the category of VR hardware. VR world-building programs allow participants to manipulate their environment within a simulation.

Today, some personal computers are fully capable of running basic VR simulations. Add-on computer boards that contain special processors for graphics rendering and signal processing can be incorporated into such basic computers. These add-ons speed up and improve the quality of graphics and audio that a VR system can provide.

Input devices, such as mice, wands, and datagloves, are the means by which a VR system receives information from the participant. This information pertains to navigation through the simulation and manipulation of objects that exist in that world. A performance specification known as six degrees of freedom (6DOF) represents the control that input devices are capable of extending within simulations. Special 6DOF input devices are used to control movement associated with changes in the participant's position and orientation.

World-building software creates virtual reality applications. These applications are commonly referred to as virtual worlds. *World-building* consists of modeling and rendering objects, assigning behaviors to those objects, incorporating interactivity, and programming. *Object-oriented programming* (OOP) has had a very favorable impact on the development of VR applications. This type of programming breaks segments of code into self-contained objects that are reusable and can be easily ported between different types of computers. Object-oriented programming languages, such as C++, are practical tools for creating virtual worlds, because they allow the programmer to write code in a modular fashion. This feature allows for greater flexibility than standard programming techniques.

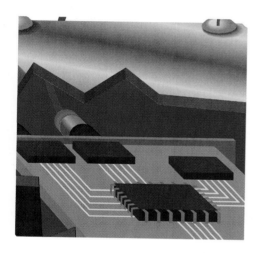

Computer Power

A *"REALITY ENGINE"* IS the heart of any virtual reality system, because it processes and generates virtual worlds. It can consist of a single computer or a group of computers. In either case, a reality engine follows software instructions in order to assemble, process, and display all the data involved in creating a virtual world. This data includes all information sent to or coming from the participant, along with any data already stored in the VR system.

The reality engine must be powerful enough to process and generate virtual worlds. This type of processing must be done in "real time" in order to avoid a lag between the participant's movements and the reality engine's response to those movements. VR programs can run on personal computers, workstations, and supercomputers. *Personal computers* consist of a microprocessor, or central processing unit (CPU). They also include peripheral devices such as a monitor, keyboard, floppy disk drive, hard disk, and often a CD-ROM drive. In the context of VR, personal computers typically are used in low-end systems, largely because they have limited graphics and sound capacities in comparison to workstations and supercomputers.

Workstations, or *minicomputers,* are high-performance computers. They are driven by powerful microprocessors and are usually based on the UNIX operating system. Workstations that are designed as reality engines for VR systems have multiple processors to further add to their overall power and performance. These systems are commonly used to develop VR applications in professional fields such as medicine, architecture, and engineering.

Supercomputers have more than one processor. In fact, these computers are also known as *multiprocessors.* They use a parallel processing architecture that can allow more than 100 processors to work on a program simultaneously, which optimizes the performance of a VR system. This processing capacity clearly distinguishes supercomputers as high-end systems. Universities, the federal government, and research labs use supercomputers in order to conduct VR experiments.

The computer in a VR system handles three types of tasks: data input, data output, and virtual-world management and generation. Keyboards, mice, forceballs, gloves, and so on are typical data input devices that are used in VR systems. These devices often rely on a *preprocessor* to translate raw data into a format the computer can accept. A preprocessor's main function is transferring data from the main processor to a second processor, which allows VR software to run faster. Preprocessing might take place on a special add-on card for a personal computer, on a second computer, or on a separate processor in a supercomputer.

Generating and processing graphics and audio output for VR systems involves considerable processing time. This is especially true of rendering. *Rendering* is the means by which a computer-generated graphic object is given details that make it more realistic. It takes into account physical characteristics of objects, such as texture and coloring. Add-in computer boards, separate processors, or even separate computers may be required to handle rendering.

Audio processing uses an internal or external sound-generating device to create and play different sounds within the virtual environment.

Virtual Reality Systems

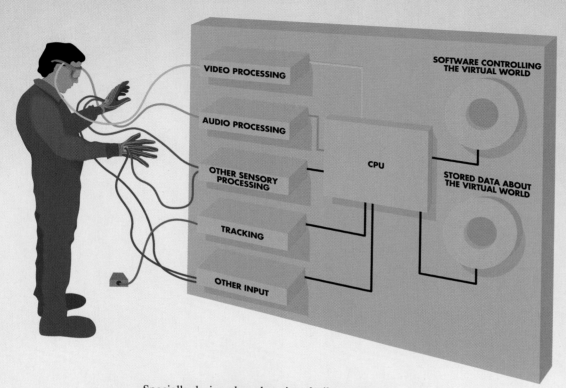

VIDEO PROCESSING

AUDIO PROCESSING

OTHER SENSORY PROCESSING

TRACKING

OTHER INPUT

CPU

SOFTWARE CONTROLLING THE VIRTUAL WORLD

STORED DATA ABOUT THE VIRTUAL WORLD

Specially designed workstations built around powerful microprocessor chips are well suited to high-end VR applications.

Microprocessor chip

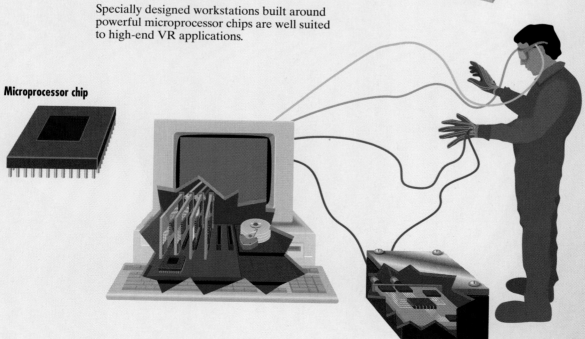

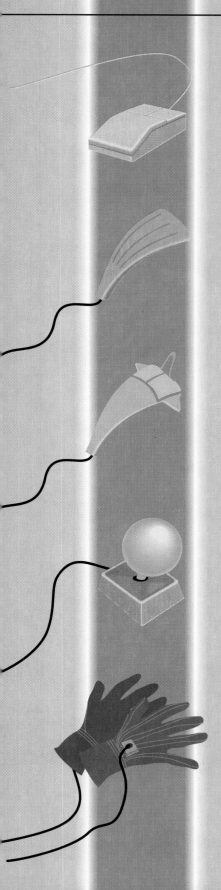

2-D Mouse   A standard computer mouse is a two degree of freedom (2DOF) input device. Most 2-D mice are electromechanical. The mouse rolls a small ball along a desk, which moves two roller bars inside the mouse. The roller bars are connected to a slotted wheel placed between a light emitting diode (LED) and a photo receptor. The rotating wheel interrupts the beam of light between the LED and the photo receptor. The movement of the ball is translated into signals that represent the direction of the mouse's movements in two dimensions, X and Y. A trackball is similar to a mouse, except the ball is stationary, and the user moves the ball with his or her hands.

Flying Mouse   A flying mouse is similar to a standard computer mouse, but when lifted off the desktop, it becomes a 6DOF sensor. Most flying mice have electromagnetic sensors built into the mouse. The Logitech 3D flying mouse uses built-in ultrasonic receivers and a stationary base with transmitters to measure the position and orientation of the mouse when it is lifted from a table. The receivers can also be used for voice input into the VR system.

Wand   A wand contains a position-tracking sensor and several buttons, and is designed to be held upright in the hand. A wand is similar to a flying mouse, except it lacks the mouse ball—the part of a mouse that rolls on the desktop.

Forceball   One of the problems with wands and flying mice is the user must continually hold the devices in their hands. Forceballs are a desktop device that still can provide up to six degrees of freedom. Forceballs, also called torque balls, are mounted on a small, stationary platform. They can be twisted, squeezed, pressed down or pulled up, and turned from side to side. Forceballs often use LEDs and photoreceptors inside the base to measure force.

Dataglove   A dataglove can capture the relative movement of the fingers, thumb, and wrist, providing signals the VR system can work with in a virtual world. The dataglove allows the hand to grasp, move, or otherwise interact with virtual objects. Datagloves also include a 6DOF position sensor, so the actual location and orientation of the hand can also be tracked.

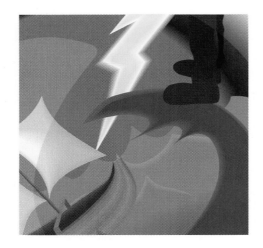

Virtual Reality Software

V R SOFTWARE PACKAGES are usually called world-building programs. *World-building* involves designing the landscape and objects a participant encounters in a virtual world. A VR programmer must take into account behavioral characteristics of the objects that exist in that world. The programmer must then incorporate this information into the actual virtual world, or *application*.

Graphics programs or computer-aided design (CAD) programs are used to model objects that appear in virtual worlds. Modeling involves creating a *wireframe,* or sketch in which all sides and components of an object are outlined, even those parts that will be hidden when the object is filled in. Rendering, which was discussed in Chapter 6, adds textures, color, and shadows, and otherwise fills out the appearance of an object.

VR *toolkits* are used to combine 3-D objects and virtual worlds and assign their characteristics. For example, a VR toolkit handles the functionality behind opening a door, turning on a fan, or playing a musical instrument within a virtual world. Many VR world-building toolkits include libraries of preexisting program code. These toolkits are based on a modular approach toward programming that lends itself well to the development of VR applications. C++ is the language of choice for most VR programmers.

World-building toolkits with *graphical user interfaces* (GUIs) enable people who lack programming skills to create virtual worlds. Within this environment, the user can insert predefined objects into the world or easily build (model) their own 3-D objects. Objects are available in libraries of 3-D clip art, or they can be imported from CAD programs. The user can then assign behaviors to the objects.

VR programmers must also be ever aware of the critical role of interactivity in developing a virtual world. Sound and portals are two aspects of interactivity that a VR programmer draws upon in creating a winning application. Chapter 4 discussed how engaging the sense of sound lends authenticity to a VR experience. Sound effects or music might be triggered by a specific event or at a particular time within a simulation. *Portals* allow transitions between environments; when the participant traverses one programmed portal, he or she passes through another environment or level within the simulation.

Creating Virtual Worlds

Virtual reality toolkits contain libraries of program functions and objects that let you create an application. Such libraries may include functions for importing geometric objects from computer-aided design (CAD) programs into the program that generates a virtual world. VR toolkits also allow the programmer to assign behaviors to objects within that world.

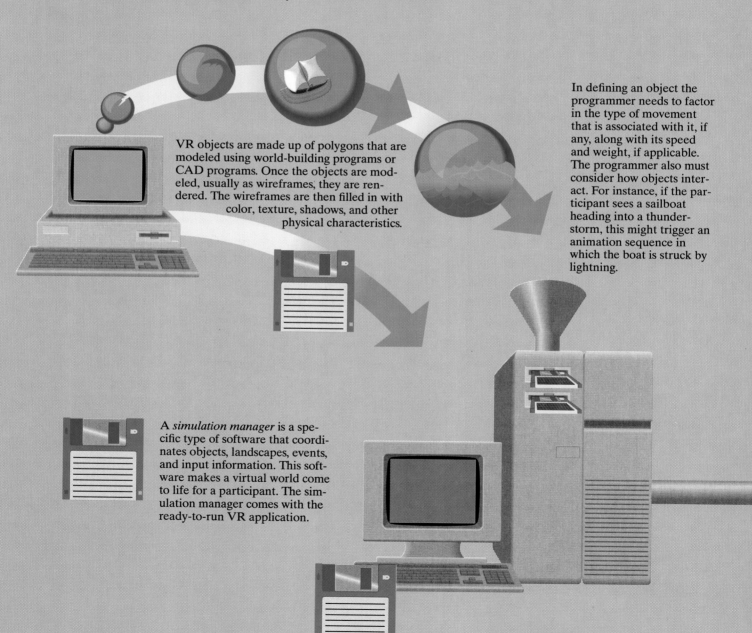

VR objects are made up of polygons that are modeled using world-building programs or CAD programs. Once the objects are modeled, usually as wireframes, they are rendered. The wireframes are then filled in with color, texture, shadows, and other physical characteristics.

In defining an object the programmer needs to factor in the type of movement that is associated with it, if any, along with its speed and weight, if applicable. The programmer also must consider how objects interact. For instance, if the participant sees a sailboat heading into a thunderstorm, this might trigger an animation sequence in which the boat is struck by lightning.

A *simulation manager* is a specific type of software that coordinates objects, landscapes, events, and input information. This software makes a virtual world come to life for a participant. The simulation manager comes with the ready-to-run VR application.

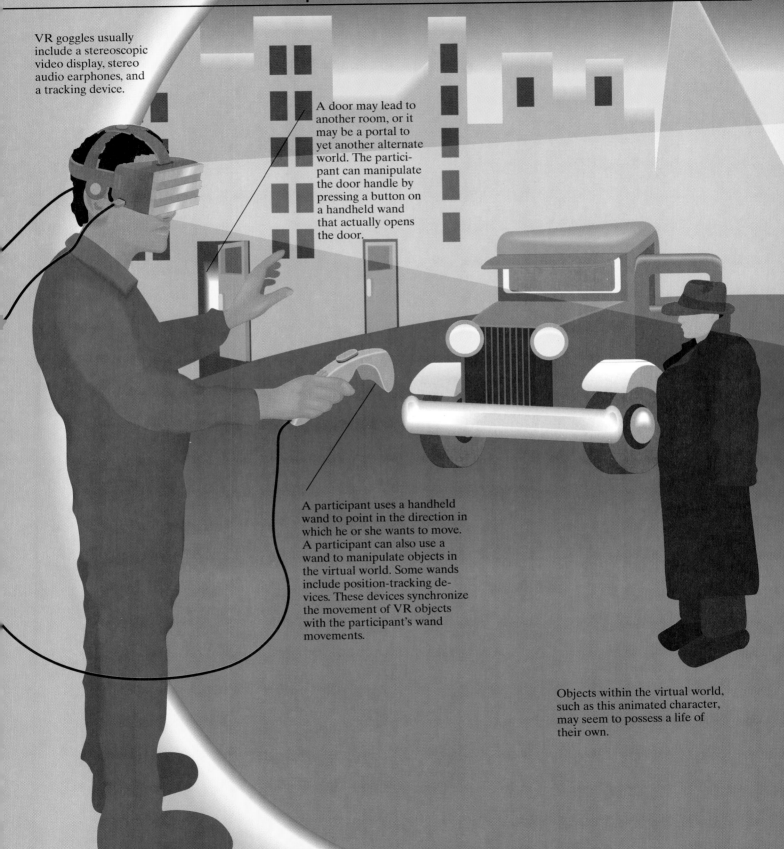

VR goggles usually include a stereoscopic video display, stereo audio earphones, and a tracking device.

A door may lead to another room, or it may be a portal to yet another alternate world. The participant can manipulate the door handle by pressing a button on a handheld wand that actually opens the door.

A participant uses a handheld wand to point in the direction in which he or she wants to move. A participant can also use a wand to manipulate objects in the virtual world. Some wands include position-tracking devices. These devices synchronize the movement of VR objects with the participant's wand movements.

Objects within the virtual world, such as this animated character, may seem to possess a life of their own.

4

DEGREES OF EXPERIENCE

CONTENTS

OVERVIEW

NTERACTIVITY AND IMMERSION are the two characteristics essential to any virtual reality experience. Consequently, VR can be divided into realms, or degrees of experience, according to which characteristics they draw upon.

Proto-VR experiences fall into the category that may have one or two characteristics of VR, but lack the requisite technical and theoretical components. An IMAX film shown in an Omnimax theater is an example of a proto-VR experience. These theaters contain a 180-degree curved screen, which serves to partially immerse an observer's sense of sight and sound into the image that is projected onto the screen. This technology can even invoke a sensation of falling or movement by means of visual cues alone. However, IMAX films lack an interactive component; neither do they qualify as simulations, because as films, they depict aspects of our normal, objective reality.

This section covers the following degrees of VR experience: desktop VR, immersion, and augmented reality. Desktop VR involves the use of personal computers and workstations to create simulations. Special software walk-throughs allow participants to design environments within simulations.

Immersion systems rely heavily on hardware such as head-mounted displays (HMDs), cab simulators, and projection VR equipment. Telepresence is an important subset of immersion. It is the means by which an operator in a given site becomes immersed in a process or procedure that is taking place at another site in real time.

Finally, augmented reality is the means by which an operator's perceptions of the real world are enhanced. This is accomplished by means of transparent HMDs that superimpose computer graphics over objects in the participant's immediate environment.

This list of degrees of experience represents the major categories of VR that are possible today. However, as the technology continues to develop, this list will expand.

Desktop Virtual Reality

DESKTOP VIRTUAL REALITY is the use of personal computers and low-end workstations to create simulations. The computer screen serves as a window through which the participant views a virtual world. Peripherals such as mice, trackballs, or forceballs are typically used to navigate the virtual world. These devices also facilitate the manipulation of objects that reside within the virtual landscape. Desktop VR lacks the full immersion capability of a head-mounted display (HMD). However, desktop VR is still popular because of its relative affordability.

Desktop VR and higher-end VR systems differ in the degrees of immersion that a participant experiences. Desktop VR systems require the participant to use a position tracker and another manual input device such as a 6DOF mouse, joystick, or forceball. These tools allow the participant to view all 360 degrees of the virtual world through the window of the computer screen while seated in front of the monitor. However, the participant does not experience full immersion because he or she can still be distracted by surroundings in the real world.

High-end VR systems employ HMDs, position trackers, other manual input devices, and sound to fully immerse the participant in a virtual world. When a participant wears an HMD, the real world is more effectively screened out and the simulation is more authentic than the desktop VR experience.

Stereoscopic effects enhance the sense of immersion in a desktop VR simulation. Devices such as inexpensive 3-D glasses, stereoscopic viewers that mount on the computer screen, and LCD shutter glasses create an illusion of three-dimensional space. These factors make desktop VR viable for business applications, particularly in the fields of engineering, architecture, and science.

Desktop VR software walk-throughs allow the participant to create a landscape or structure, such as a building, and then navigate the resulting virtual environment. Objects within the world cannot be assigned interactive behaviors, so the participant moves through the virtual world as an observer, lacking the ability to change or affect any aspect of the world. These programs, which are easy to use, are filling niches in a spectrum of fields from architecture to movie production. In the film industry, such programs allow set designers to test configurations before proceeding with actual construction.

Virtual Reality and the Desktop

Desktop VR programs are popular today even though they don't offer the full immersion effect achievable with head-mounted displays (HMDs) and other expensive VR equipment. Desktop VR produces a virtual world that the participant can view through the window of a computer screen. The participant can also navigate this world and sometimes interact with the simulated environment.

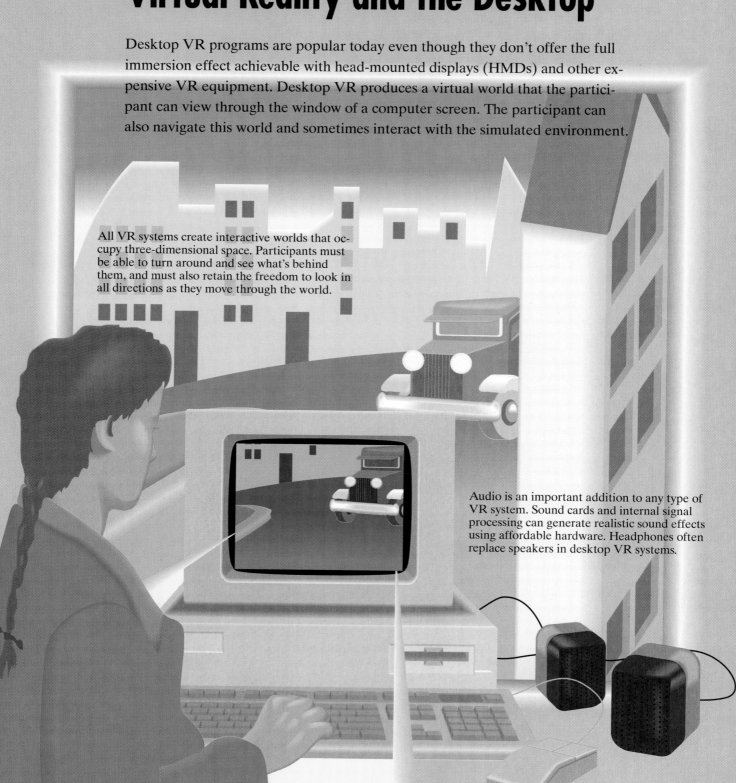

All VR systems create interactive worlds that occupy three-dimensional space. Participants must be able to turn around and see what's behind them, and must also retain the freedom to look in all directions as they move through the world.

Audio is an important addition to any type of VR system. Sound cards and internal signal processing can generate realistic sound effects using affordable hardware. Headphones often replace speakers in desktop VR systems.

Desktop VR systems use many input devices. However, not all devices or functions will work with all applications. Compatibility depends on whether the software developer included the necessary software drivers, or instructions, for individual devices.

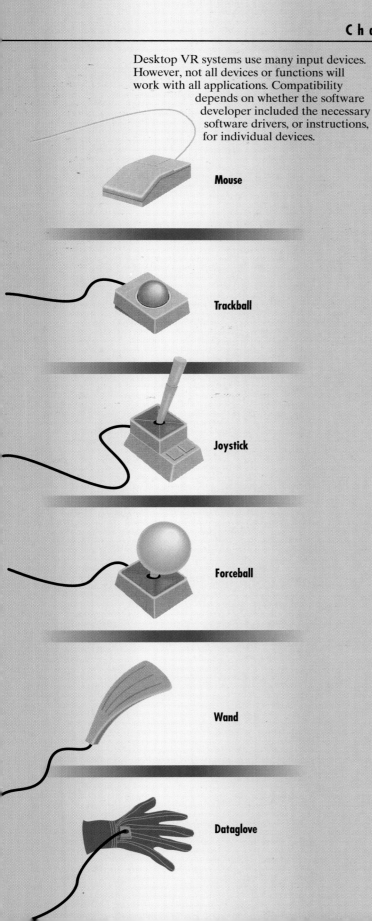

Mouse

Trackball

Joystick

Forceball

Wand

Dataglove

Many output devices can be used with a desktop monitor to create a stereoscopic effect. This effect helps the participant feel that he or she is immersed in a three-dimensional virtual world.

3-D glasses use a red and blue colored lens to combine images of the same colors into one stereoscopic image. Some even use polarized lenses to combine polarized images.

LCD shutter glasses are synchronized to the alternating display of two separate images on a monitor. When the right-side image is shown, the shutter over the left eye is closed, and the one over the right eye is opened. When the second image is shown, the left eye's shutter opens, and the one over the right eye closes. If this process happens quickly enough, at least 60 times per second per eye, the brain interprets the resulting images as a single, stereoscopic view.

A viewer containing optics fits over the computer screen. Optics combine two images generated side by side on a screen into stereoscopic images for each eye. Optics allow the participant to focus on the computer screen at a close range, and they increase the field of view of images displayed on the screen.

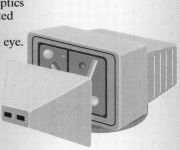

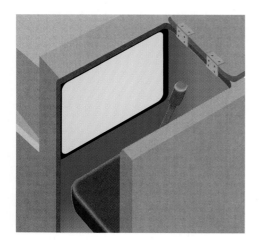

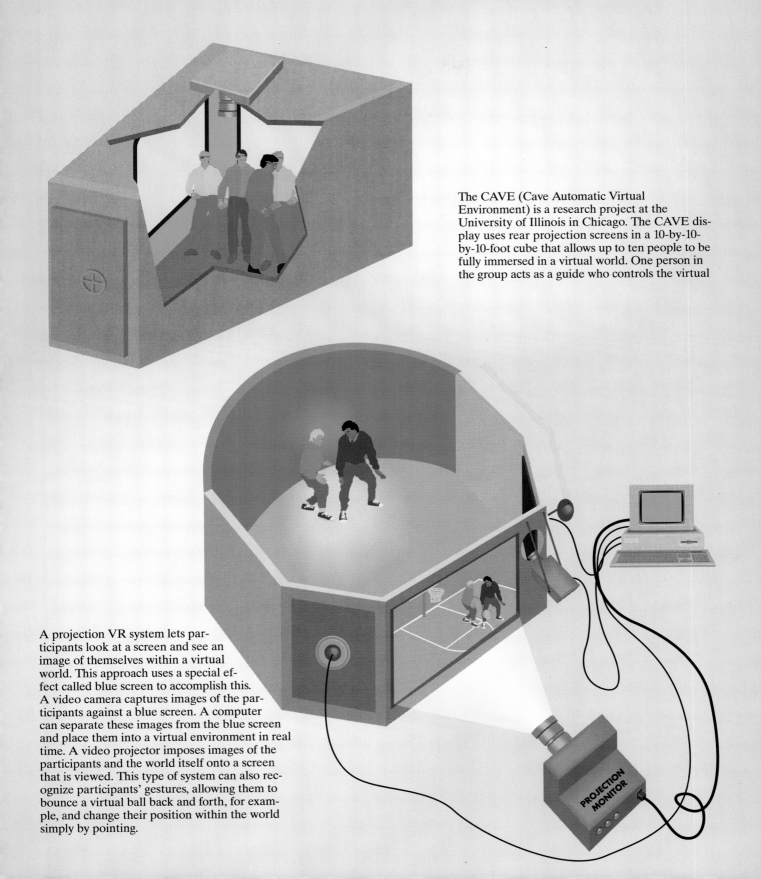

The CAVE (Cave Automatic Virtual Environment) is a research project at the University of Illinois in Chicago. The CAVE display uses rear projection screens in a 10-by-10-by-10-foot cube that allows up to ten people to be fully immersed in a virtual world. One person in the group acts as a guide who controls the virtual

A projection VR system lets participants look at a screen and see an image of themselves within a virtual world. This approach uses a special effect called blue screen to accomplish this. A video camera captures images of the participants against a blue screen. A computer can separate these images from the blue screen and place them into a virtual environment in real time. A video projector imposes images of the participants and the world itself onto a screen that is viewed. This type of system can also recognize participants' gestures, allowing them to bounce a virtual ball back and forth, for example, and change their position within the world simply by pointing.

PROJECTION MONITOR

Telepresence and Performance Animation Systems

Telepresence is a form of immersion that involves remote control. An operator may wear a head-mounted display (HMD) and use input devices that are similar to those used in virtual reality, to remotely control a robotic device. Performance animation systems (PAS) can be categorized as types of telepresence systems and VR systems. PAS's use VR tracking devices to capture an actor or operator's motion, allowing that motion to be transferred to a computer-generated cartoon image. Some television commercials are the products of PAS technology.

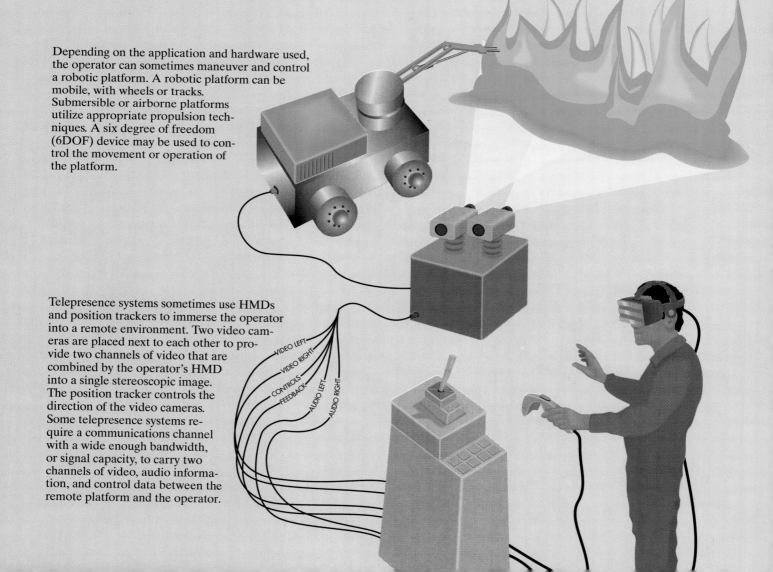

Depending on the application and hardware used, the operator can sometimes maneuver and control a robotic platform. A robotic platform can be mobile, with wheels or tracks. Submersible or airborne platforms utilize appropriate propulsion techniques. A six degree of freedom (6DOF) device may be used to control the movement or operation of the platform.

Telepresence systems sometimes use HMDs and position trackers to immerse the operator into a remote environment. Two video cameras are placed next to each other to provide two channels of video that are combined by the operator's HMD into a single stereoscopic image. The position tracker controls the direction of the video cameras. Some telepresence systems require a communications channel with a wide enough bandwidth, or signal capacity, to carry two channels of video, audio information, and control data between the remote platform and the operator.

VIDEO LEFT
VIDEO RIGHT
CONTROLS
FEEDBACK
AUDIO LEFT
AUDIO RIGHT

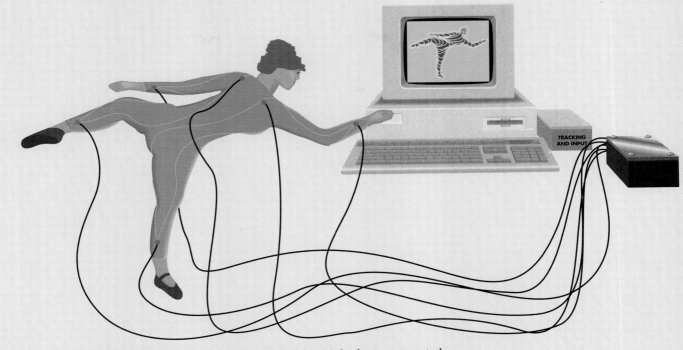

Active-tracking sensors placed on the participant's body are connected by wires to the PAS. The sensors record and communicate data about the participant's movements to the PAS. These movements are then displayed on the computer monitor in real time.

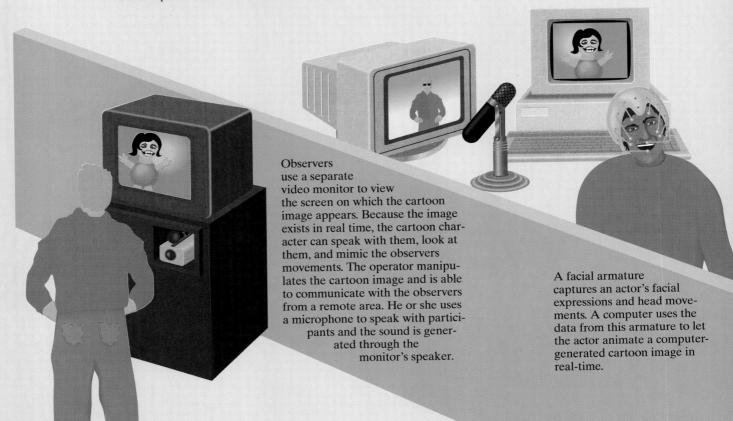

Observers use a separate video monitor to view the screen on which the cartoon image appears. Because the image exists in real time, the cartoon character can speak with them, look at them, and mimic the observers movements. The operator manipulates the cartoon image and is able to communicate with the observers from a remote area. He or she uses a microphone to speak with participants and the sound is generated through the monitor's speaker.

A facial armature captures an actor's facial expressions and head movements. A computer uses the data from this armature to let the actor animate a computer-generated cartoon image in real-time.

The operator sees instructions and
images superimposed against the
actual devices he or she is manipulating.

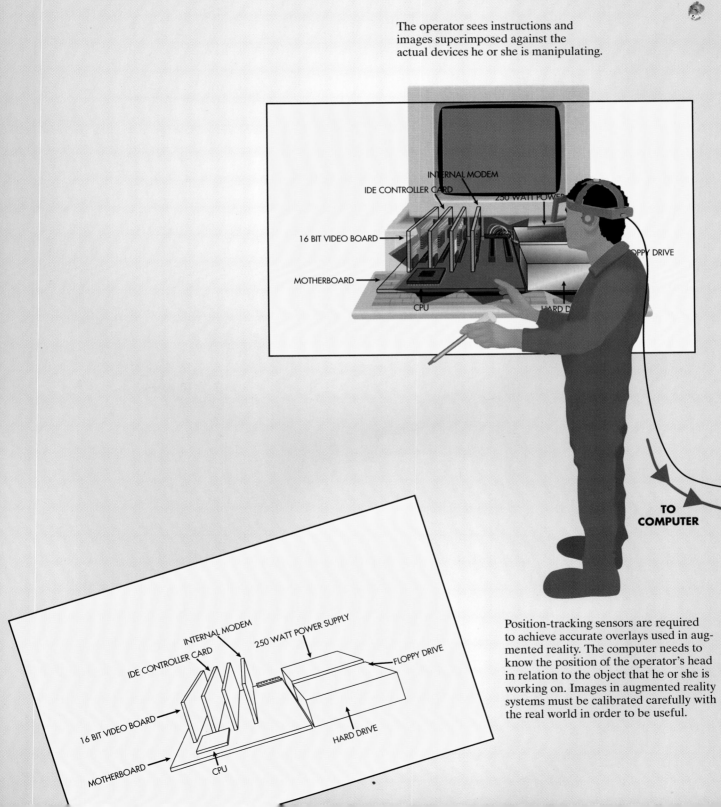

INTERNAL MODEM

IDE CONTROLLER CARD

250 WATT POWER

16 BIT VIDEO BOARD

FLOPPY DRIVE

MOTHERBOARD

CPU

HARD D

**TO
COMPUTER**

INTERNAL MODEM

IDE CONTROLLER CARD

250 WATT POWER SUPPLY

FLOPPY DRIVE

16 BIT VIDEO BOARD

HARD DRIVE

MOTHERBOARD

CPU

Position-tracking sensors are required
to achieve accurate overlays used in augmented reality. The computer needs to
know the position of the operator's head
in relation to the object that he or she is
working on. Images in augmented reality
systems must be calibrated carefully with
the real world in order to be useful.

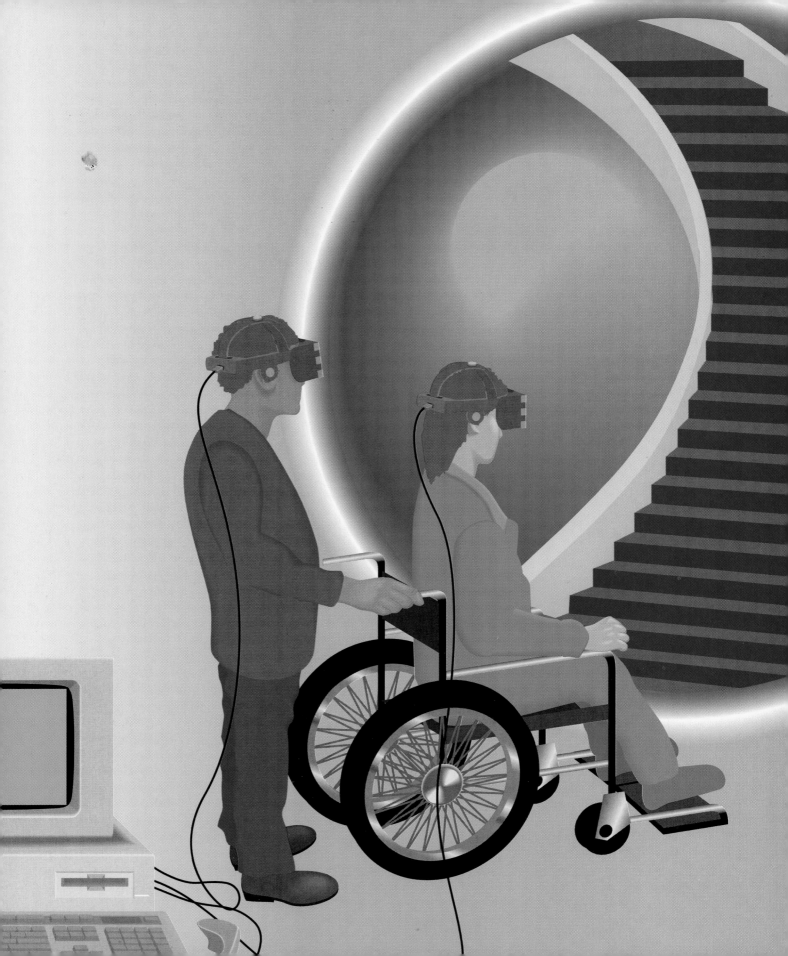

PROFESSIONAL APPLICATIONS

CONTENTS

PROFESSIONAL AND SCIENTIFIC applications for virtual reality are actually more widespread than recreational applications. Although relatively expensive, VR technology can be cost effective in many professional applications.

VR technology is being used in fields as diverse as medicine, architecture and engineering, military research, science, and financial analysis. In medical VR applications, students can learn anatomy by dissecting a virtual cadaver or follow a blood cell through the valves of a heart. Doctors use simulations of data scanned from a real patient to plan operations or other procedures. Biochemists manipulate molecular building blocks, watching a stereoscopic image of different drugs and biochemicals reacting when combined. Soon such medical procedures as *telesurgery*, or surgery conducted from a remote location, may be commonplace.

Virtual reality has had an equally strong impact on the fields of architecture and engineering. Architects can use CAD (computer-aided design) tools to design and model a building, and then transfer the resulting database to a VR system. Prospective clients can then use HMDs and 6DOF (six degrees of freedom) devices to navigate through a virtual mock-up of a building. The architect can change the colors of walls, reposition furniture or location of windows in real time, showing the client different versions of the architectural design. City planners can show how a proposed building will affect a skyline. Rules of physical behavior—weight, elasticity, and structural integrity—can be programmed into a virtual world, allowing engineers to test products before building prototypes.

Virtual reality technology is based upon military flight simulators, and it is still used in this field. The military has built networked battlefield simulations that link various tank and aircraft simulators across the world into a single virtual theater of war. NASA also uses VR aircraft and spaceship simulators as standard applications to create simulations of telerobotic equipment for interplanetary exploration.

Visualization, an established subset of computer applications closely related to VR, is based on the old saying "A picture is worth a thousand words." Visualization condenses massive amounts of numerical and analytical data from computer models into graphical images that scientists, financial analysts, and other professionals can explore visually. For example, scientific visualization applications employ VR technology to immerse a scientist into a virtual environment, allowing him or her to explore data relationships visually. VR scientific visualizations have been used for modeling supersonic airflow across the wings of aircraft, for modeling the geology of oil fields to maximize oil production, and for astrophysics research. Scientific visualization is also a useful tool for explaining complex environmental problems to nonscientists.

Financial visualization can be used to model massive amounts of data that changes constantly. Financial modeling creates a virtual representation of a company or industry. Different sets of data within a company, such as production figures, employment, or sales, can be represented by objects located in a virtual environment. Managers and investors can navigate through this data, examining individual items or detecting overall trends.

Current VR applications for financial visualization fall into two major areas: financial modeling of businesses and industries, and visualization of financial markets such as Wall Street. Brokers and investment professionals buy, sell, and trade in the financial markets, and to do so successfully, they need to keep track of constantly fluctuating information about interest rates, bonds, mutual funds, and stock market prices. These complex markets require the latest and most powerful tools to assist traders and investment professionals in making money in a competitive environment. Financial professionals use HMDs and other handheld devices to gather information about stock markets into a single visual environment, where they can navigate through the data, looking for patterns, deals, and fast-moving stocks to invest in.

The increasing use of VR technology is inevitable as the prices of input and output devices come down, video display quality increases, and powerful yet easy-to-use software becomes available.

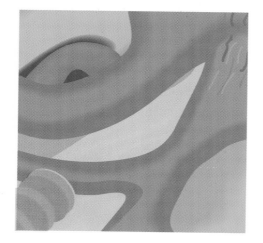

Medical Applications

VIRTUAL REALITY HAS begun to have a significant impact in the field of medicine. This field is in the early stages of harnessing VR technology to create applications ranging from molecular modeling of synthetic drugs to simulations for teaching anatomy and surgery.

Today, computers are often used to design synthetic drugs. VR simulators such as the Grope III, which is in use at the University of North Carolina at Chapel Hill, allow researchers to test the properties of new drugs. Grope III enables researchers to see and feel how molecules within a drug interact with other biochemicals. This type of sophisticated technology accelerates the process of developing drugs for a wide variety of health problems.

VR applications for medicine combine conventional two-dimensional images generated by CAT (computerized axial tomography) scans or MRI (magnetic resonance imaging) with stereoscopic images. These images can be viewed with VR goggles or on screens with the assistance of stereoscopic shutter glasses. Doctors can use this technology to make diagnoses without performing invasive medical procedures.

VR technology can also provide simulations of human anatomy. Instead of being limited to reading books or working on cadavers, medical students can work on a virtual patient in order to understand the complexities of human anatomy. Surgical simulations are similar to anatomical simulations. However, they incorporate more properties and behaviors into the organs and flesh. This enables the surgeon to interact with the body in order to move, repair, or remove tissues and organs. Position-tracking sensors are attached to scalpels and scissors, monitoring and recording the surgeon's position and orientation for the VR system. The surgeon wears VR goggles, which display a stereoscopic view of a virtual body with a working musculoskeletal system and a complete interactive organ system, functioning in the same fashion as their real-life counterparts.

Surgical simulators allow surgeons to practice their skills before a difficult operation and to maintain their skills over time. Surgeons are able to rehearse for various medical scenarios, perhaps using real imagery gathered from characteristics of a specific patient. These dress rehearsals give doctors a better chance of success when it comes time to operate on live patients.

Virtual Surgery

Surgeons use virtual reality to practice difficult surgeries before operating on live patients. If real imagery from the patient is fed into the simulation from CAT, MRI, or other imaging technology, the surgeon can plan the actual surgery accordingly. This allows him or her to anticipate complications that might otherwise have been unexpected. Virtual surgery also gives new doctors the opportunity to rehearse operations they've never performed before.

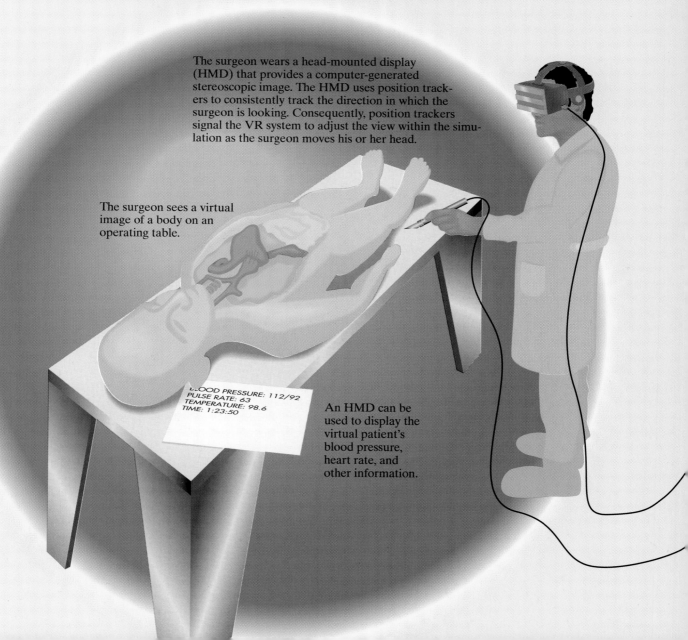

The surgeon wears a head-mounted display (HMD) that provides a computer-generated stereoscopic image. The HMD uses position trackers to consistently track the direction in which the surgeon is looking. Consequently, position trackers signal the VR system to adjust the view within the simulation as the surgeon moves his or her head.

The surgeon sees a virtual image of a body on an operating table.

BLOOD PRESSURE: 112/92
PULSE RATE: 63
TEMPERATURE: 98.6
TIME: 1:23:50

An HMD can be used to display the virtual patient's blood pressure, heart rate, and other information.

Position-tracking devices are placed on the surgical instruments the doctor uses. This allows the VR system to accurately track body movement and position, as well as surgical interaction between the doctor and the virtual body. Handheld devices that mimic surgical instruments while providing force feedback are under development. They will provide realistic resistance to scalpels and other instruments as they move through virtual flesh.

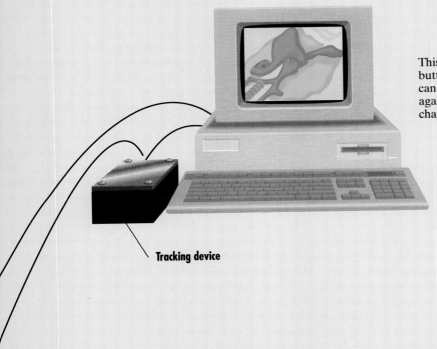

Tracking device

This is a simulation, so the doctor can press an undo button and back up. If the virtual patient dies, he or she can be instantly resuscitated, and the surgeon can start again. The surgeon gains experience that increases the chances of success during a real operation.

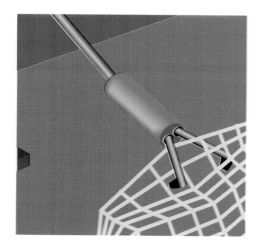

Engineering and Architecture

THE FIELDS OF engineering and architecture have begun to accept virtual reality as a unique development tool. VR is currently being used to design products and construction equipment, to set up factories, and even to arrange products on display in simulations for retail stores.

The various aspects of prototyping, design, and production processes have traditionally involved a number of discrete steps that did not allow electronic data to be shared. This often resulted in the duplication of efforts. As programs for computer systems such as *CAD* (computer-aided design), *CAE* (computer-aided engineering), and *CAM* (computer-aided manufacturing) have become standardized, these steps have increasingly been linked into one system. For example, the same database can be used to create a VR simulation for prototyping, engineering, and production line design.

The automotive industry is a pioneer in adopting VR technology. The process of designing a new car on paper to finishing a production model can take years; VR technology is shortening this time frame. In the past, the new car design was modeled out of clay. The initial design required many subsequent stages of work to develop the basic look, check aerodynamics, and adjust passenger ergonomics. VR simplifies these steps through the creation of simulations from a database that is gathered from CAD and CAE programs. This database contains data about the final version of a car design.

In VR applications for the automotive industry, a technician tries to assemble car parts in a simulation. The technician can make sure the parts fit together properly before time and money are spent creating the actual parts. VR can also be used to design and simulate an assembly line setup. This type of simulation would represent the machinery that is used to assemble parts to test whether it can do so properly and in the right order without interfering with other equipment. As with parts assembly, using a simulation of an assembly line setup also saves time and money in the long run.

Architecture is another field in which VR is making an impact. An architect can take CAD data of a house or building and convert it into a simulation that might include faucets with running water, light switches, door handles, and so on. The architect can also modify lighting, heating, and acoustics within the simulation. By using an HMD and a pointing device, an architect can guide a prospective client into a simulation. The HMD allows the client to see interior space from various angles while navigating the building. The pointing device is the key to repositioning windows and widening or narrowing door-ways in real time. Any changes made during the tour are automatically recorded into a database, so the architect's final set of drawings will reflect revisions without further input.

These elaborate architectural simulations also allow architects to make sure a de-sign meets handicapped accessibility rules. For example, a person in a wheelchair can wear an HMD and attach position sensors to the chair in order to explore a virtual building. This kind of approach makes it easy to identify design errors in counter height, passageways, or other unforeseen problems.

The Automotive Industry and Virtual Reality

The automotive industry is just starting to use VR technology to design and build cars. It can take two years or more to advance from the development of an initial concept for a new type of car to the moment a production version rolls off the assembly line. VR technology promises to shorten this cycle greatly, reducing the need for physical mockups. This same technology allows the same 3-D database to hold data about each component as it progresses through every stage of the design phase.

A simulation allows company officials, engineers, and technicians to make decisions about a car's shape, check how parts fit together, and see the final product without building mockups of parts or of the entire car.

VR allows engineers to set up workstations on the assembly line as simulations. Using the same database that contains the car's original design, engineers can resolve potential part-assembly conflicts. VR significantly accelerates this process by streamlining every phase from concept to actual production.

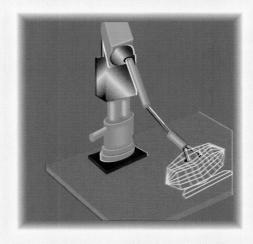

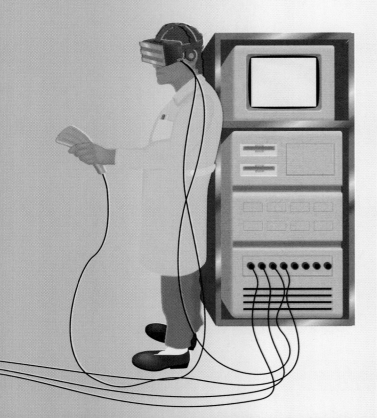

Large-scale computer systems handle the calculations and database for automotive design from the beginning of the process through assembly on the production line. These systems rely on mainframes, engineering workstations, and networks.

Architecture and Virtual Reality

Virtual reality expands the results of two-dimensional and three-dimensional CAD modeling into 3-D spaces that an architect or client can explore and interact with. Virtual houses, hospitals, office buildings, and any other spaces that a CAD program can model can be used in a simulation. Architects can use HMDs or flat screens to explore these virtual environments.

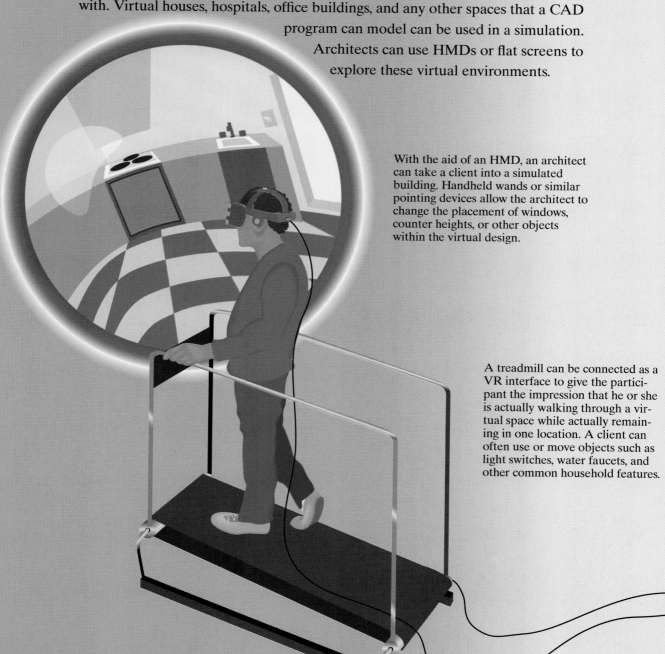

With the aid of an HMD, an architect can take a client into a simulated building. Handheld wands or similar pointing devices allow the architect to change the placement of windows, counter heights, or other objects within the virtual design.

A treadmill can be connected as a VR interface to give the participant the impression that he or she is actually walking through a virtual space while actually remaining in one location. A client can often use or move objects such as light switches, water faucets, and other common household features.

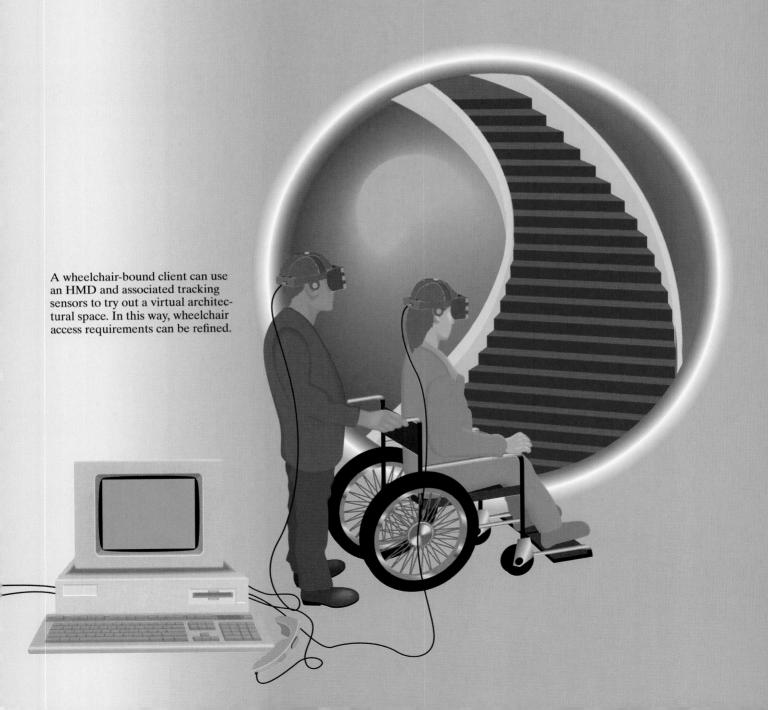

A wheelchair-bound client can use an HMD and associated tracking sensors to try out a virtual architectural space. In this way, wheelchair access requirements can be refined.

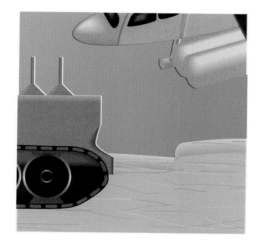

Simnet provided a protocol, or common way of interchanging information, so that various types of simulators could use the same types of data. Pods simulating tanks, armored troop carriers, helicopters, and jet fighters can share the same virtual space.

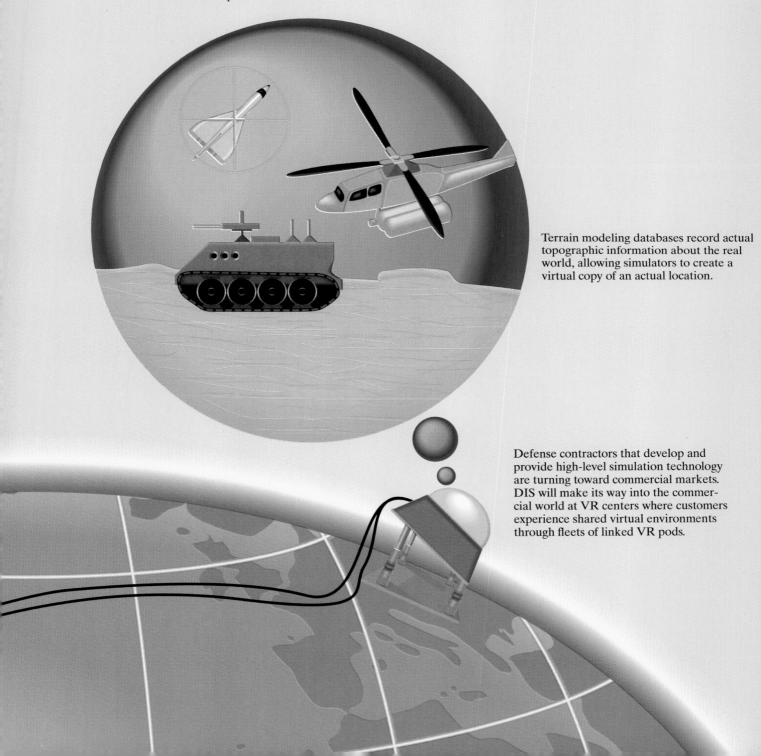

Terrain modeling databases record actual topographic information about the real world, allowing simulators to create a virtual copy of an actual location.

Defense contractors that develop and provide high-level simulation technology are turning toward commercial markets. DIS will make its way into the commercial world at VR centers where customers experience shared virtual environments through fleets of linked VR pods.

Commercial Aviation and Flight Simulators

Commercial aviation has benefited from the post-World War II introduction of flight simulators. Pilots train with flight simulators to learn how to operate commercial jets without risking passengers' lives. These simulators also avoid the costs that are associated with an actual flight. Many airlines require pilots to take an annual refresher course in flight simulators.

FLIGHT SIMULATOR

Most commercial flight simulators utilize pods, which are often built on hydraulic motion platforms. Computer-generated screens serve as cockpit windows that are used to project the virtual environment. A simulator interfaces the same cockpit controls and instruments that are found in a real airplane. Some flight simulators include head-mounted displays (HMDs) to generate the image of the cockpit controls, which makes for a very complete VR simulation.

Because flight simulators can be programmed, a pilot can practice a greater number of types of takeoffs and landings than possible in a real airplane. In addition, a pilot can simulate scenarios that are rarely encountered or survived in a real airplane, such as wind shear, near misses with other aircraft, and loss of engine power or other kinds of mechanical failure. By practicing for these scenarios in a simulator, the pilot's and passengers' chances of surviving such an event in real life are increased.

Researchers can use flight simulators to observe the impact of different drugs on pilots and aircraft crew. Commercial research is being conducted on the effects of prescription medicines and drugs such as caffeine and alcohol. Military researchers also test the reactions of crews to drugs that counteract chemical warfare agents.

CHAPTER
16

Scientific Visualization

SCIENTIFIC VISUALIZATION TRANSLATES massive amounts of alphanumeric data into images that are easier to interpret than raw data alone. Virtual reality applications in this field allow the participant to move forward and backward in time and space and to examine data that can be seen in visible light, infrared light, and in microwave radar images. This is all accomplished by means of VR input devices such as 6DOF mice or wands, which are used to switch sets of data that are germane to each aspect of the simulation. The GROPE project at the University of North Carolina at Chapel Hill is an example of an innovative approach to scientific visualization. GROPE allows a researcher to use a robotic arm in order to interact with virtual molecules.

Scientific visualization draws on data arising from many sources. For example, satellites and airplanes use *remote sensing* to gather gigabytes (billions of bytes) of data about the earth and other planets. Once such data is collected, it is converted into images, which may be infrared and radar visuals of the atmosphere, ocean, and land. *Direct sensing* is the mechanism for compiling data about temperature, wind speed and direction, and rainfall. This data pertains to places that are on the surface of the earth.

Electron microscopes and medical scanners are other sources of data for scientific visualization. Supercomputers are another source; they are used often to create mathematical models of molecules, earthquakes, and components of the earth's environment. Molecular modeling may be used to test how different molecules react with each other. Seismic models are used to study plate tectonics and earthquakes. Environmental modeling can plot the impact of the effacement of the ozone layer and the effects of global warming over a period of time. Each of these models generates massive amounts of statistical data. Scientific visualization is often the only way to interpret this data.

Scientific Visualization

Virtual reality has been used for molecular modeling, astrophysics, engineering, and large-scale environmental research. This illustration shows how VR can be used to interpret data gathered from many sources as it pertains to a single region of the earth.

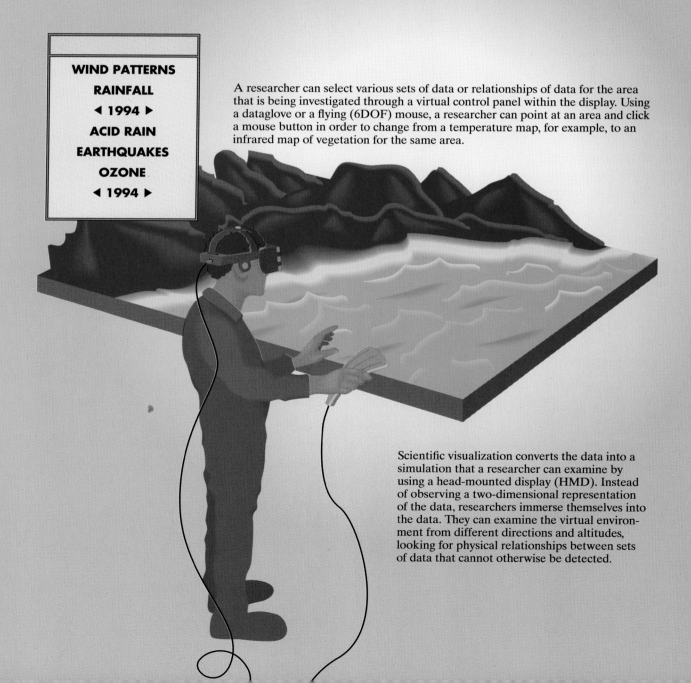

WIND PATTERNS

RAINFALL

◄ 1994 ►

ACID RAIN

EARTHQUAKES

OZONE

◄ 1994 ►

A researcher can select various sets of data or relationships of data for the area that is being investigated through a virtual control panel within the display. Using a dataglove or a flying (6DOF) mouse, a researcher can point at an area and click a mouse button in order to change from a temperature map, for example, to an infrared map of vegetation for the same area.

Scientific visualization converts the data into a simulation that a researcher can examine by using a head-mounted display (HMD). Instead of observing a two-dimensional representation of the data, researchers immerse themselves into the data. They can examine the virtual environment from different directions and altitudes, looking for physical relationships between sets of data that cannot otherwise be detected.

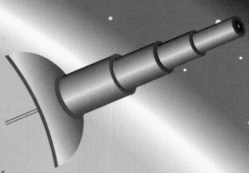

Remote sensing from satellites, the space shuttle, or high-altitude aircraft is used to gather various types of images about the atmosphere, ocean, and land. Infrared and radar images are two kinds of graphics that can be generated. Ground-based sensors collect information about temperature, wind speed and direction, and rainfall.

A researcher can also use the Fakespace Labs' binocular omni-orientation monitor BOOM display to view a scientific visualization. The BOOM is a stereoscopic monitor that is set up on a jointed support arm. The view on the BOOM is linked to the support arm, so it changes as the BOOM is moved. BOOM provides a simple way for a researcher working at a desk to become immersed in a virtual world.

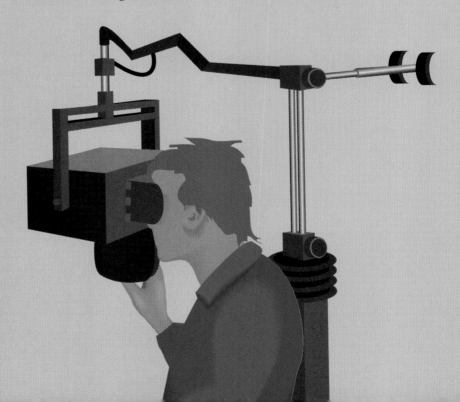

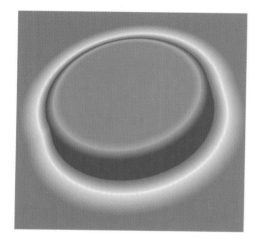

Financial Visualization

LIKE ITS SCIENTIFIC counterpart, financial visualization converts large amounts of alphanumeric data into graphics or visual objects, making the data easier to interpret and analyze. The stock market is the principal industry that takes advantage of this technology.

The stock market made the transition from paper transactions to electronic ones in the 1970s. Since then, the daily volume and complexity of financial markets have increased tremendously. Many institutional investors can now trade entire portfolios, or collections of securities and bonds, at one time.

The Metaphor Mixer was the first financial visualization application for VR. It was developed for Maxus Systems International in New York City. Reuters Select sends current financial information via satellite, which the Metaphor Mixer gathers and presents to the broker within a virtual environment in real time. The environment resembles a virtual football field. Grid lines divide companies into industry groups by category. The companies are further divided by market, such as the American Stock Exchange, Tokyo Stock Market, Hong Kong Exchange, Los Angeles Stock Exchange, and so on. This product is currently used by professionals rather than by consumers.

When using the Metaphor Mixer, the broker wears a head-mounted display (HMD) in order to become immersed in a simulation of the financial marketplace. An input device, such as a hand-held wand or forceball, allows the broker to move through the simulation and access information about various companies.

Companies are represented by colored "poker chips." Each chip's color symbolizes a type of financial activity. For example, red chips indicate prices that have dropped since the previous day, blue chips signify a raise in price, and gray chips represent a stable price. The number of chips in a stack convey the relative trading price of the stock. Spinning and blinking chips represent selective criteria about each company that brokers can analyze.

Avatar Partners, located in Boulder Creek, California, offers the vrTrader for Windows-based financial visualization, for use by consumers and professionals. This application uses 3-D objects, real-time graphs, and text within its virtual environment. *Alerts,* which are visual and auditory cues, signal the user about significant events in the market. The color and behavior of objects changes according to important developments.

For a product like vrTrader to be useful, the flow of stock market data must be nearly instantaneous. In this case, a network control center transmits market information directly by satellite to FM radio or to individual satellite dishes for further broadcasting. A dedicated signal receiver box transfers current information to the user's computer.

Small price variations between different markets such as the American Stock Exchange and the Tokyo Stock Exchange mean the difference between losing money and making a profit. Financial visualization applications are a viable means of accessing current data in an industry that changes by the minute.

The Virtual Stock Market

Virtual reality combines complex data about many stock markets into a single virtual world. A trader or broker uses stereoscopic shutter glasses or a head-mounted display (HMD) and an input device to enter and interact with this world. He or she can navigate through this simulation, detect relationships between stocks and markets, and absorb massive amounts of information at a glance. Financial visualization applications are an effective way of gaining and maintaining an edge in a very competitive market.

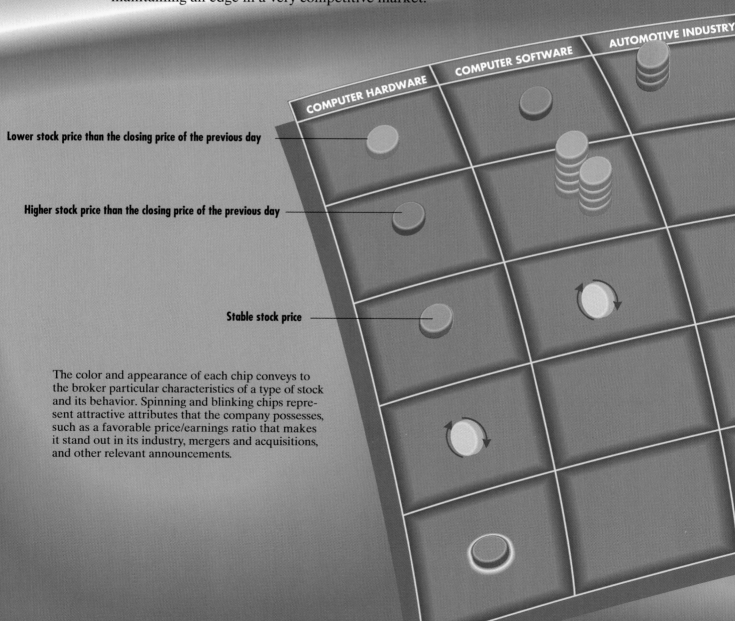

Lower stock price than the closing price of the previous day

Higher stock price than the closing price of the previous day

Stable stock price

The color and appearance of each chip conveys to the broker particular characteristics of a type of stock and its behavior. Spinning and blinking chips represent attractive attributes that the company possesses, such as a favorable price/earnings ratio that makes it stand out in its industry, mergers and acquisitions, and other relevant announcements.

The Metaphor Mixer uses "poker chips" to represent companies in a simulated financial marketplace. The environment resembles a football field. Grid lines are superimposed over the field, separating one company from another.

The virtual stock market can be viewed on a computer screen. However, the broker can experience full immersion by wearing an HMD equipped with a position tracker. He or she can then freely navigate within the virtual world.

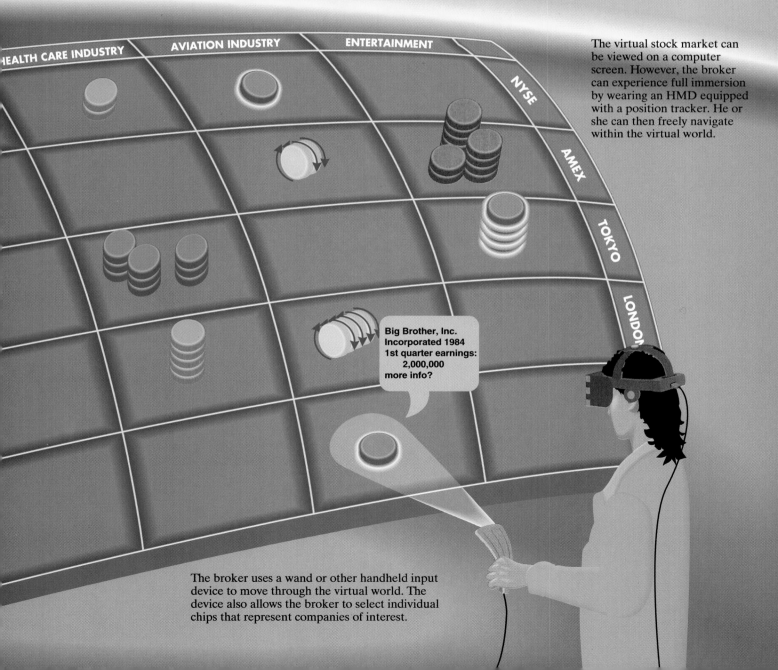

HEALTH CARE INDUSTRY

AVIATION INDUSTRY

ENTERTAINMENT

NYSE

AMEX

TOKYO

LONDON

**Big Brother, Inc.
Incorporated 1984
1st quarter earnings:
2,000,000
more info?**

The broker uses a wand or other handheld input device to move through the virtual world. The device also allows the broker to select individual chips that represent companies of interest.

Once inside the virtual world, the player is free to navigate through it and interact with the objects it contains. There are usually many ways to win these games.

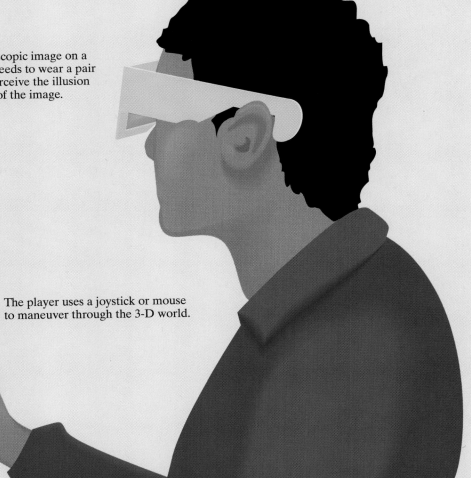

Some games create a stereoscopic image on a single monitor. The player needs to wear a pair of 3-D glasses in order to perceive the illusion of width, height, and depth of the image.

The player uses a joystick or mouse to maneuver through the 3-D world.

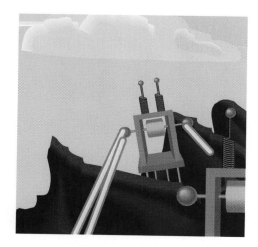

Virtual Reality in Entertainment

AFTER SITTING THROUGH a pre-mission briefing, you climb into a cab known as a Mech and power up the system. You see other Mechs through a viewport that snaps onto the cab. Some of them are operated by friends and others by foes. The nearest one engages you in a laser battle. Your Mech is hit and explodes, as your virtual persona ejects in an escape pod. You then rejoin the fight in a brand new Mech. The battle continues until the game is over.

You've been interacting in real time with other players in a computer-generated 3-D simulation. It's *BattleTech*, a simulator that the public can play at the Virtual World Center in Chicago. Commercial VR entertainment has grown into a multimillion-dollar industry since the introduction of *BattleTech* in 1991. Today you can fight air battles in the Hornet-1 jet simulator by Magic Edge of Mountain View, California, or experience the latest in VR games in Las Vegas. Systems are also planned to open at other sites across the country within the next few years. On average, it costs consumers a dollar a minute to play a fully immersive VR game. The games last from 3 to 20 minutes.

These games are only cost effective when they are used at a public site, where the games' programmability and throughput are maximized. Programmability is key to upgrading games once they've become obsolete. Throughput allows multiple customers to use a system per hour or within the same day.

VR games utilize variations of hardware discussed earlier in this book. Almost all of these VR platforms can be used individually or networked in cyberspace, a shared environment where a group of participants coexist within the same virtual world.

The quality of graphics that you will find in immersive VR systems varies according to the amount of computer power that is available to the graphic artist. Very high-end graphics require supercomputers; some systems can only generate cartoon quality graphics.

The degree and prevalence of violence in all types of VR games has generated growing concern. The more immersive simulations may have a negative influence on the player's normal behavior. While earlier immersive VR games were based on violent activities, there is an increasing trend to offer peaceful solutions. Cooperative, team-based scenarios are also becoming more common.

Commercial VR Entertainment

You can find entertainment based on virtual reality technology at many public sites throughout the country. Many of the games at these entertainment centers are networked, allowing multiple players to enter the same virtual world simultaneously. Players are pitted against each other or against computer-generated opponents. To win, the player must use a unique combination of wit, logic, and hand/eye coordination while immersed in the virtual world.

Depending on the type of simulation, players see graphical representations of other players, or they may just see their vehicles.

Group experiences often involve a briefing, or orientation. Most games cannot be mastered in a single session but require multiple trips through the simulation.

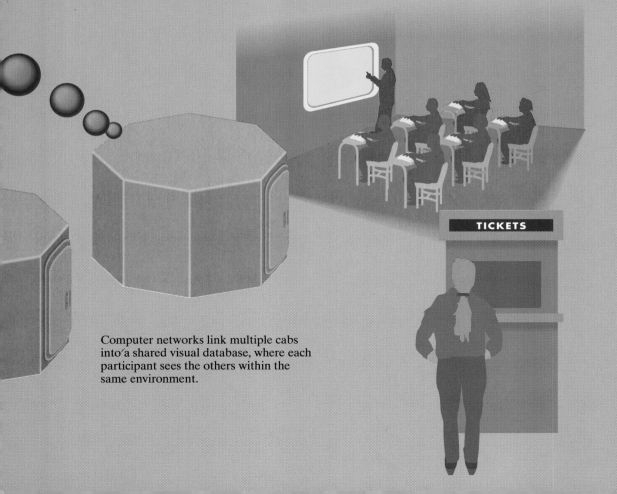

Computer networks link multiple cabs into a shared visual database, where each participant sees the others within the same environment.

TICKETS

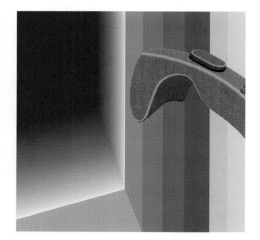

Art and Virtual Reality

MYRON KRUEGER IS an arts scholar whose work over the last 25 years has defined much of what is considered aesthetic in the realm of virtual reality. He has designed installations known as *responsive environments,* which use computer and video technology. Krueger coined the term "artificial reality" to describe his responsive environments.

GLOWFLOW is an example of a responsive environment. It debuted in 1969 as Krueger's first example of projection VR. The *GLOWFLOW* responsive environment consisted of hidden minicomputers, sound synthesizers, and series of tubes with phosphorescent multicolored fluids, which were used to create a dynamic atmosphere of visual effects. This environment immersed participants without their personal use of any special equipment, such as head-mounted displays. After *GLOWFLOW*, Krueger went on to develop *METAPLAY*, *PSYCHIC SPACE*, and *VIDEO-PLACE*. Each successive responsive environment was increasingly complex, requiring more intricate interfaces between computer graphics, video, and audio.

In 1993, the Guggenheim Museum in the SoHo section of New York City exhibited five virtual worlds. Artist Thomas Dolby's work, *Virtual String Quartet*, allowed a participant to interact with virtual musicians. The participant could change the rhythm of the music simply by changing his or her physical location. In order to change the music, the participant merely had to interact with the virtual musician.

Artist Jenny Holzer's *World 1* was also exhibited at the Guggenheim. Her work allowed the participant to interact with images and sounds that she associated with war-torn Bosnia.

The *Networked Virtual Art Museum*, created by artist Carl Loeffler, was another work that was exhibited at the Guggenheim. Participants wore head-mounted displays (HMDs) to browse through the halls of the museum, examining artworks and architecture.

One criterion commonly applied to art is the degree to which it is innovative, and virtual reality is a medium that alows for extensive innovations. It is an apt vehicle for artists because of its overall flexibility as a communication medium.

The Arts and Virtual Reality

There are several natural relationships that exist between the arts and virtual reality technology. Like VR, art can be immersive and concern itself with simulations in its efforts to imitate life. Artists can use VR to engage our senses in order to provide us with an aesthetic experience.

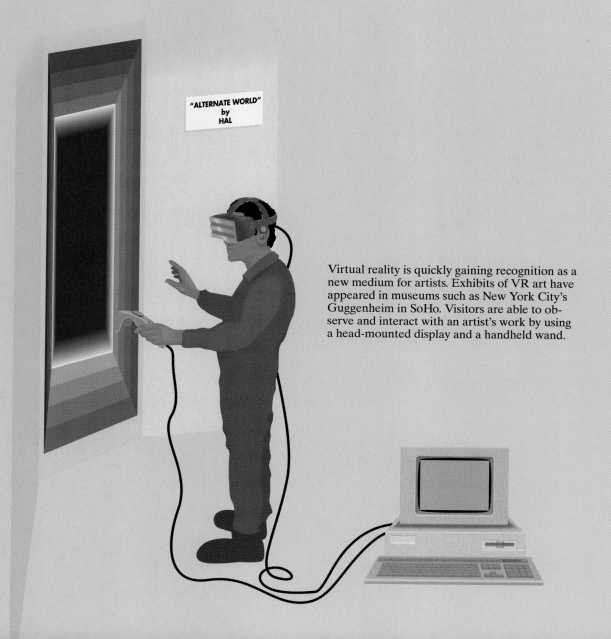

"ALTERNATE WORLD"
by
HAL

Virtual reality is quickly gaining recognition as a new medium for artists. Exhibits of VR art have appeared in museums such as New York City's Guggenheim in SoHo. Visitors are able to observe and interact with an artist's work by using a head-mounted display and a handheld wand.

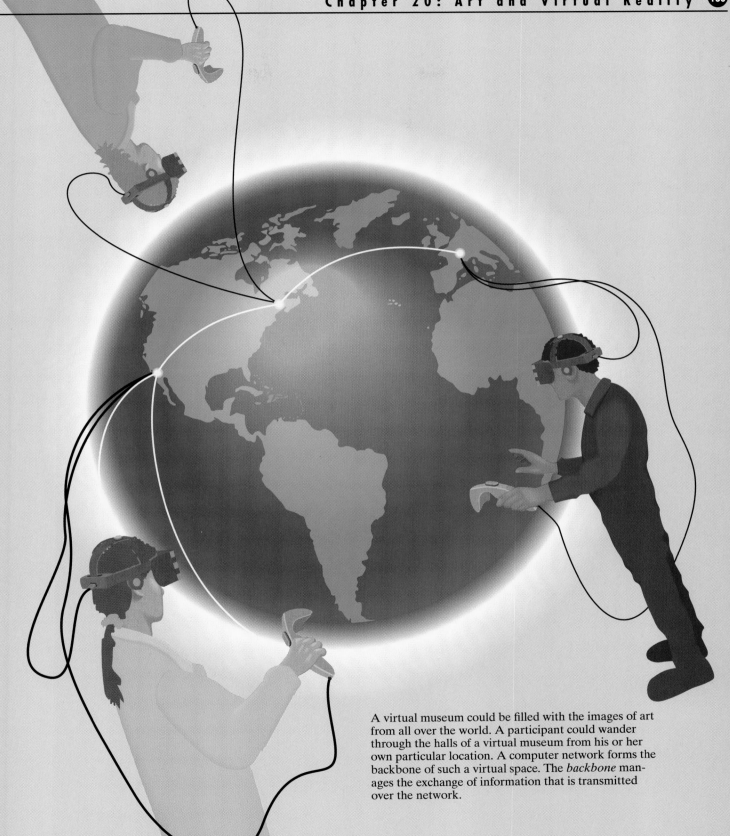

A virtual museum could be filled with the images of art from all over the world. A participant could wander through the halls of a virtual museum from his or her own particular location. A computer network forms the backbone of such a virtual space. The *backbone* manages the exchange of information that is transmitted over the network.

The teacher could use a handheld wand to escort the students through the virtual world, observing key points in a critical encounter. The teacher could also change the course of history as a means of encouraging discussion about historic facts. With inclusion of VR in the classroom, students can look forward to visiting other countries, planets, and centuries.

CHAPTER

22

Disabilities and Virtual Reality

SOME DAY, VIRTUAL reality may allow people with disabilities to access a cyberspace community, unhindered by their physical limitations that exist in the real world. VR is proving to be an effective tool for helping some individuals with disabilities overcome obstacles posed by their immediate environment. For example, Chapter 14 discussed how a person in a wheelchair can go on a walk-through of a proposed structure to evaluate handicap accessibility.

Applications that deal with specific disabilities such as cerebral palsy are also being developed. The Oregon Research Institute in Eugene, for instance, uses VR to teach children how to navigate a motorized wheelchair. The trainees usually consist of children with disabilities that inhibit the ability to walk. The child wears a head-mounted display (HMD), and the wheelchair is mounted on a rolling platform. The child uses a joystick connected to the wheelchair to navigate through a virtual world without having to worry about running into obstacles.

The Human Interface Technology (HIT) lab in Seattle uses a VR application designed specifically for people with Alzheimer's disease. People in this population often lose their ability to walk independently, because the brain becomes incapable of sending the necessary signals to the legs. However, if the subject can use an augmented reality HMD to see virtual lines overlaid on the real floor, he or she can follow them in order to attempt to retain or regain the ability to walk.

VR programs can also mimic psychological or physiological disabilities, helping specialists in these fields gain a clearer sense of what living with them entails. For example, autism is a poorly understood neurological condition that causes significant communication difficulties. As some children in this population grow older, a certain number of them are able to learn communication skills, which enable them to tell us firsthand about the symptoms of this disease. These symptoms include impaired vision and hearing as well as exaggerated tactile and olfactory senses. If VR technology can be used to simulate the ways in which autism affects the senses, it may lead to effective ways of overcoming aspects of this disability.

Current VR applications for overcoming disabilities hold a great deal of promise. The obvious potential in this field is likely to encourage more exploration.

Overcoming Disabilities with Virtual Reality

Virtual reality can provide ingenious solutions for some of the problems facing people with disabilities. For example, at the Oregon Research Institute, children use VR to learn how to operate motorized wheelchairs. Likewise, the Human Interface Technology (HIT) lab in Seattle uses a VR application designed to help people with Alzheimer's disease.

A technician monitors the simulation and can offer encouragement to the child.

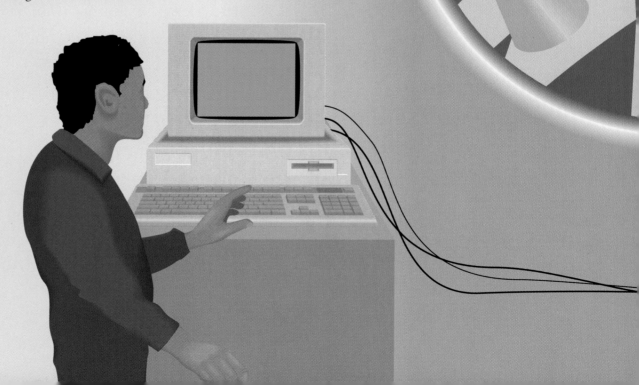

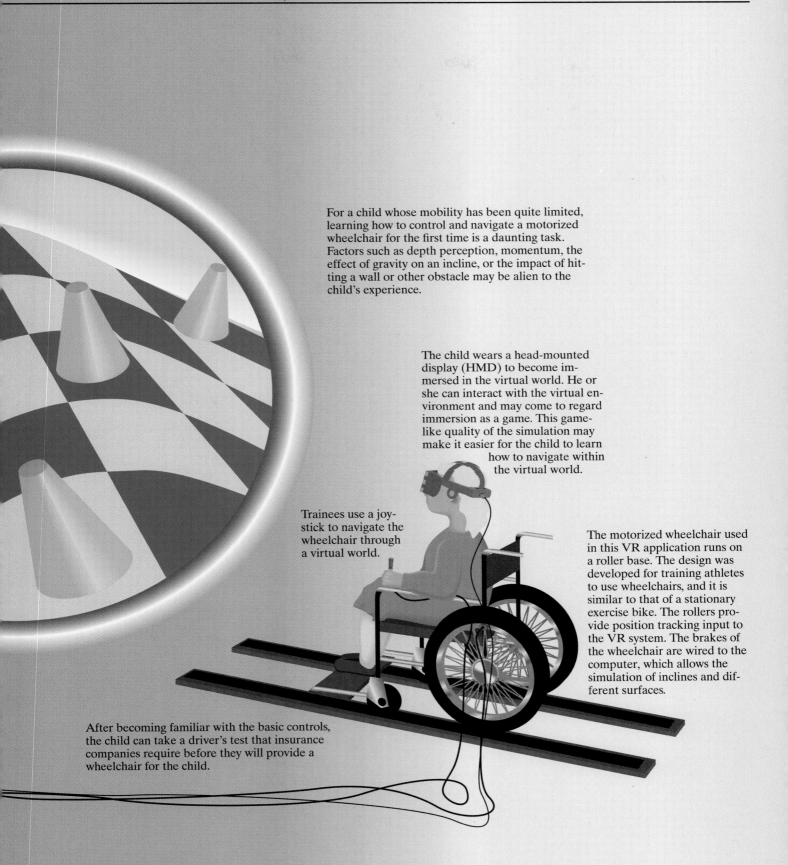

For a child whose mobility has been quite limited, learning how to control and navigate a motorized wheelchair for the first time is a daunting task. Factors such as depth perception, momentum, the effect of gravity on an incline, or the impact of hitting a wall or other obstacle may be alien to the child's experience.

The child wears a head-mounted display (HMD) to become immersed in the virtual world. He or she can interact with the virtual environment and may come to regard immersion as a game. This game-like quality of the simulation may make it easier for the child to learn how to navigate within the virtual world.

Trainees use a joystick to navigate the wheelchair through a virtual world.

The motorized wheelchair used in this VR application runs on a roller base. The design was developed for training athletes to use wheelchairs, and it is similar to that of a stationary exercise bike. The rollers provide position tracking input to the VR system. The brakes of the wheelchair are wired to the computer, which allows the simulation of inclines and different surfaces.

After becoming familiar with the basic controls, the child can take a driver's test that insurance companies require before they will provide a wheelchair for the child.

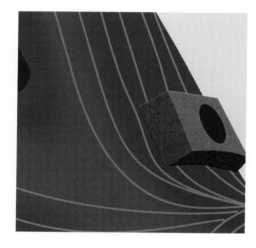

The Future of Virtual Reality

WHILE VIRTUAL REALITY technology is currently mature enough to be used in practical applications in many fields, it is still clearly in its early developmental phase. In many ways, it is still a technology that we are just beginning to learn how to apply. However, it is easy to project the path of its continued evolution: It will include faster and higher quality graphics, more affordable and better designed head-mounted displays (HMDs), other input and output devices, and faster computer processing power. These enhancements will influence various aspects of VR applications, from the visual and audio quality of virtual worlds, to the breadth of VR applications that will be available in new fields. In addition, new technologies will revolutionize VR, such as in the field of haptics (the study of the sense of touch) where researchers are currently investigating how touch could be incorporated into VR.

Artificial intelligence (AI) is another area of computer technology that may well push VR into new directions. AI involves programming computers to simulate human thinking processes. An AI *expert system* consists of a database or collection of rules on a specific topic. This information is gleaned from a real-life expert.

AI *agents* already serve as guides or assistants who provide information to VR participants, functioning much like an animated help function. An agent may appear as a "talking head" or it could be represented as a full figure in a virtual environment. For example, a player of a VR game could ask an agent for help or for hints on how to win the game. The agent might respond verbally or simply act out a reply. An agent in a medical application might provide a second opinion to a doctor working on a difficult surgical procedure.

A-life, or artificial life, is a branch of AI. A-life forms appear to be alive and they interact with participants in virtual worlds. A-life agents are being used in VR research laboratories.

The ability of users to share virtual worlds on a global scale will create virtual communities in cyberspace. These real-time interactions promise unlimited opportunities for people from diverse cultures to communicate and pool their collective knowledge. In future developments in VR, the line between *virtual* reality and *reality* may become less discernible.

New Hardware Technologies

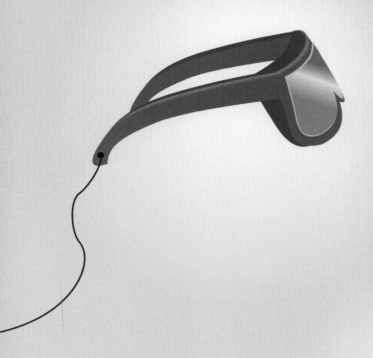

Head-mounted displays (HMDs) may soon be indistinguishable from sunglasses. New HMDs are developed every six months. With each generation, the resolution improves, the weight decreases, and the cost becomes more affordable.

Researchers have experimented with body suits designed to collect data about the position and orientation of a participant's body. Body suits that provide sensory input to the entire body do not yet exist.

ATTENTION TEACHERS AND TRAINERS
Now You Can Teach From These Books!

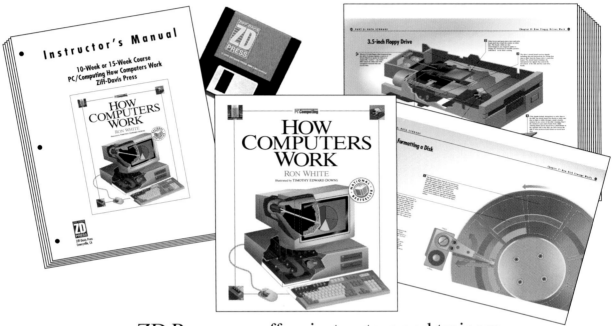

ZD Press now offers instructors and trainers
the materials they need to use these books in their classes.

- An Instructor's Manual features flexible lessons designed for use in a 10- or 15-week course (30-45 course hours).

- Student exercises and tests on floppy disk provide you with an easy way to tailor and/or duplicate tests as you need them.

- A Transparency Package contains all the graphics from the book, each on a single, full-color transparency.

- Spanish edition of *PC/Computing How Computers Work* will be available.

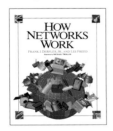

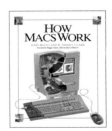

ZIFF-DAVIS
ZD PRESS

See.

It's that simple.

Just open these colorfully illustrated guide-books and watch the answers to your software questions unfold.

The HOW TO USE books from Ziff-Davis Press make computing easy by presenting each task visually on two facing pages. You'll see what you want to achieve, and exactly how to achieve it.

There's no guess work. The HOW TO USE books are the affordable alternative for those of us who would rather let the computer do the work.

For more information call (800)688-0448, ext. 208.

There is a book for every major software package, with new titles publishing every month.

How to Use the Mouse in Windows

An *input device* is a means of giving instructions to the computer. You're probably familiar with the keyboard as the most common input device. A *mouse*, so named for its hunched-over appearance and tail-like cable, is a hand-held input device that along with the keyboard is one of the two input devices most people use routinely in Windows. Although it's possible to get by without a mouse and do all your work from the keyboard, it's not too wise. The Windows interface was designed with the mouse in mind. Keyboard alternatives can be awkward—and it's not always easy to find out what they are. Take a few minutes to learn the major mouse moves and you'll reward yourself with smoother computing.

The mouse pointer is on the Write program icon.

Click here to pull down the Options menu. Then click on a command. To close the menu without issuing a command, click outside the menu.

To *click* on something means to point to it (roll the mouse so the mouse pointer is on top of it) and then press and instantly release the left mouse button. To *double-click* on something means to point to it and then click the left mouse button twice in rapid succession.

Drag across a word to select it. Then press the Delete key to delete it.

1. To *roll* the mouse means to move the mouse along the tabletop without pressing one of the mouse buttons. As you roll the mouse, the *mouse pointer* on the screen moves in the same direction. You only roll the mouse to "point to" something on the screen as a prelude to another action.

5. Another way to scroll is to drag the scroll button to a new location along the scroll bar. The position of the scroll button suggests what part of the contents you are viewing.

TIP SHEET

- Unless told otherwise, use the *left* mouse button. The other mouse buttons are used so infrequently in Windows that when they are used, you're always told about it specifically.
- Some mice have two buttons, and others have three. The right mouse button is used infrequently, and the middle button on the three-button mouse is almost never used.
- For keyboard alternatives to the scroll bars and the maximize/minimize/restore buttons, turn the page.

Imagination.
Innovation. Insight.

The How It Works Series from Ziff-Davis Press

"... a magnificently seamless integration of text and graphics ..."

Larry Blasko, The Associated Press, reviewing *PC/Computing How Computers Work*

No other books bring computer technology to life like the *How It Works* series from Ziff-Davis Press. Lavish, full-color illustrations and lucid text from some of the world's top computer commentators make *How It Works* books an exciting way to explore the inner workings of PC technology.

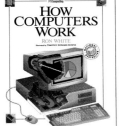

ISBN: 094-7 Price: $22.95

PC/Computing How Computers Work

A worldwide blockbuster that hit the general trade bestseller lists! *PC/Computing* magazine executive editor Ron White dismantles the PC and reveals what really makes it tick.

How Networks Work

Two of the most respected names in connectivity showcase the PC network, illustrating and explaining how each component does its magic and how they all fit together.

ISBN: 129-3 Price: $24.95

How Macs Work

A fun and fascinating voyage to the heart of the Macintosh! Two noted *MacUser* contributors cover the spectrum of Macintosh operations from startup to shutdown.

How Software Works

This dazzlingly illustrated volume from Ron White peeks inside the PC to show in full-color how software breathes life into the PC. Covers Windows™ and all major software categories.

ISBN: 133-1 Price: $24.95

ISBN: 184-6 Price: $17.95

ISBN: 146-3 Price: $24.95

How to Use Your Computer

Conquer computerphobia and see how this intricate machine truly makes life easier. Dozens of full-color graphics showcase the components of the PC and explain how to interact with them.

All About Computers

This one-of-a-kind visual guide for kids features numerous full-color illustrations and photos on every page, combined with dozens of interactive projects that reinforce computer basics, making this an exciting way to learn all about the world of computers.

How To Use Word

Make Word 6.0 for Windows Work for You!

A uniquely visual approach puts the basics of Microsoft's latest Windows-based word processor right before the reader's eyes. Colorful examples invite them to begin producing a variety of documents, quickly and easily. Truly innovative!

How To Use Excel

Make Excel 5.0 for Windows Work for You!

Covering the latest version of Excel, this visually impressive resource guides beginners to spreadsheet fluency through a full-color graphical approach that makes powerful techniques seem plain as day. Hands-on "Try It" sections give new users a chance to sharpen newfound skills.

ISBN: 155-2 Price: $22.95

ISBN: 166-8 Price: $15.95

ISBN: 185-4 Price: $17.95

Available at all fine bookstores or by calling 1-800-688-0448, ext. 100. Call for more information on the Instructor's Supplement, including transparencies for each book in the *How It Works* Series.

ZIFF-DAVIS
ZD
PRESS

The Quick and Easy Way to Learn.

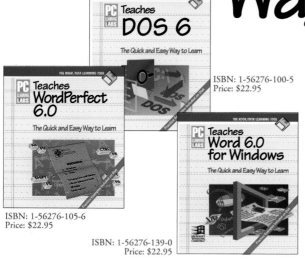

Teaches DOS 6
The Quick and Easy Way to Learn
ISBN: 1-56276-100-5
Price: $22.95

Teaches WordPerfect 6.0
The Quick and Easy Way to Learn
ISBN: 1-56276-105-6
Price: $22.95

Teaches Word 6.0 for Windows
The Quick and Easy Way to Learn
ISBN: 1-56276-139-0
Price: $22.95

We know that PC Learning Labs books are the fastest and easiest way to learn because years have been spent perfecting them. Beginners will find practice sessions that are easy to follow and reference information that is easy to find. Even the most computer-shy readers can gain confidence faster than they ever thought possible.

The time we spent designing this series translates into time saved for you. You can feel confident that the information is accurate and presented in a way that allows you to learn quickly and effectively.

ISBN: 1-56276-122-6
Price: $22.95

ISBN: 1-56276-176-5
Price: $22.95

ISBN: 1-56276-148-X
Price: $22.95

ISBN: 1-56276-135-8
Price: $22.95

ISBN: 1-56276-020-3
Price: $22.95

ISBN: 1-56276-134-X
Price: $22.95

ISBN: 1-56276-124-2
Price: $22.95

ISBN: 1-56276-074-2
Price: $22.95

ISBN: 1-56276-033-5
Price: $22.95

ISBN: 1-56276-051-3
Price: $22.95

ISBN: 1-56276-154-4
Price: $22.95

ISBN: 1-56276-138-2
Price: $22.95

ZIFF-DAVIS ZD PRESS

Also available: Titles featuring new versions of Excel, 1-2-3, Access, Microsoft Project, Ami Pro, and new applications, pending software release. Call 1-800-688-0448 for title update information.

Available at all fine bookstores, or by calling 1-800-688-0448, ext. 103.

Ziff-Davis Press Survey of Readers

Please help us in our effort to produce the best books on personal computing.
For your assistance, we would be pleased to send you a FREE catalog
featuring the complete line of Ziff-Davis Press books.

1. How did you first learn about this book?

Recommended by a friend . . . . ☐ -1 (5)

Recommended by store personnel . . . . ☐ -2

Saw in Ziff-Davis Press catalog . . . . ☐ -3

Received advertisement in the mail . . . . ☐ -4

Saw the book on bookshelf at store . . . . ☐ -5

Read book review in: _____ ☐ -6

Saw an advertisement in: _____ ☐ -7

Other (Please specify): _____ ☐ -8

2. Which THREE of the following factors most influenced your decision to purchase this book? (Please check up to THREE.)

Front or back cover information on book . . . ☐ -1 (6)

Logo of magazine affiliated with book . . . . . . ☐ -2

Special approach to the content . . . . ☐ -3

Completeness of content . . . . ☐ -4

Author's reputation. . . . . ☐ -5

Publisher's reputation . . . . ☐ -6

Book cover design or layout . . . . ☐ -7

Index or table of contents of book . . . . ☐ -8

Price of book . . . . ☐ -9

Special effects, graphics, illustrations . . . . . . ☐ -0

Other (Please specify): _____ ☐ -x

3. How many computer books have you purchased in the last six months? _____ (7-10)

4. On a scale of 1 to 5, where 5 is excellent, 4 is above average, 3 is average, 2 is below average, and 1 is poor, please rate each of the following aspects of this book below. (Please circle your answer.)

Depth/completeness of coverage	5 4 3 2 1	(11)
Organization of material	5 4 3 2 1	(12)
Ease of finding topic	5 4 3 2 1	(13)
Special features/time saving tips	5 4 3 2 1	(14)
Appropriate level of writing	5 4 3 2 1	(15)
Usefulness of table of contents	5 4 3 2 1	(16)
Usefulness of index	5 4 3 2 1	(17)
Usefulness of accompanying disk	5 4 3 2 1	(18)
Usefulness of illustrations/graphics	5 4 3 2 1	(19)
Cover design and attractiveness	5 4 3 2 1	(20)
Overall design and layout of book	5 4 3 2 1	(21)
Overall satisfaction with book	5 4 3 2 1	(22)

5. Which of the following computer publications do you read regularly; that is, 3 out of 4 issues?

Byte . . . . ☐ -1 (23)

Computer Shopper . . . . ☐ -2

Corporate Computing . . . . ☐ -3

Dr. Dobb's Journal . . . . ☐ -4

LAN Magazine . . . . ☐ -5

MacWEEK . . . . ☐ -6

MacUser . . . . ☐ -7

PC Computing . . . . ☐ -8

PC Magazine . . . . ☐ -9

PC WEEK . . . . ☐ -0

Windows Sources . . . . ☐ -x

Other (Please specify): _____ ☐ -y

Please turn page.

6. What is your level of experience with personal computers? With the subject of this book?

	With PCs	With subject of book
Beginner	☐ -1 (24)	☐ -1 (25)
Intermediate	☐ -2	☐ -2
Advanced	☐ -3	☐ -3

7. Which of the following best describes your job title?

Officer (CEO/President/VP/owner)........ ☐ -1 (26)
Director/head......................... ☐ -2
Manager/supervisor.................... ☐ -3
Administration/staff................... ☐ -4
Teacher/educator/trainer.............. ☐ -5
Lawyer/doctor/medical professional....... ☐ -6
Engineer/technician................... ☐ -7
Consultant.......................... ☐ -8
Not employed/student/retired........... ☐ -9
Other (Please specify): _____ ☐ -0

8. What is your age?

Under 20............................ ☐ -1 (27)
21-29.............................. ☐ -2
30-39.............................. ☐ -3
40-49.............................. ☐ -4
50-59.............................. ☐ -5
60 or over.......................... ☐ -6

9. Are you:

Male............................... ☐ -1 (28)
Female............................. ☐ -2

Thank you for your assistance with this important information! Please write your address below to receive our free catalog.

Name: _____

Address: _____

City/State/Zip: _____

Fold here to mail.

2303-07-08

BUSINESS REPLY MAIL
FIRST CLASS MAIL   PERMIT NO. 1612   OAKLAND, CA

POSTAGE WILL BE PAID BY ADDRESSEE

Ziff-Davis Press
ZIFF-DAVIS
ZD
PRESS
5903 Christie Avenue
Emeryville, CA 94608-1925
Attn: Marketing